4.98

THE ILLUSTRATED GUIDE TO THE HOUSES OF AMERICA

THE

ILLUSTRATED GUIDE

TO THE

HOUSES OF AMERICA

Edited by

Richard M. Ballinger

and Herman York

Galahad Books • New York City

THE ILLUSTRATED GUIDE TO THE HOUSES OF AMERICA

Library of Congress Catalog Card Number: 73-92079
ISBN 0-88365-177-7

Published by arrangement with Hawthorn Books, Inc.
Manufactured in the United States of America

Designed by Harold Franklin

CONTENTS

Richard M. Ballinger

INTRODUCTION

This book was prepared to give the reader, whether a prospective home buyer, a builder, a real-estate agent, a lender, or one of the many professionals serving the housing industry, an appreciation of the popular housing styles in America today.

Most authentic styles were developed for good functional reasons, often related to the conditions of the region in which they are found, such as the climate or the kinds of building materials abundant in the area. Today, many of these styles are just as practical in one part of the country as another.

Good design and styling in new housing are in short supply. The general public has easy access to information on interior planning and decorating, but a wide range of information on exterior styling is not readily available. Consequently, the demand for good style has suffered.

Furthermore, the cyclical nature of the industry has played a part in retarding the emergence of good house design on any sizable scale within the industry. For example, the builders of new housing immediately after World War II were building purely for the "shelter" market, a market of first-time buyers, where the only demand of the young home buyer was for maximum space at minimum cost. Good design was luxury.

Toward the end of the 1950's the majority of the new house market was made up of second-, third-, and fourth-time buyers. Most of these families could afford something better, and "quality" became a keynote of the industry. Better products, better construction, and larger and more expensive housing came more and more into evidence. A realistic upgrading in design, however, was less noticeable.

The great majority of builders continued to create their own designs or depended on "standard plans" services—some good, some bad—rather than on the services of an architect. Often the builder had no other choice, for few architects today are interested in residential design except for the most expensive custom houses. Churches, schools, and industrial and commercial construction offer more lucrative prospects. Few architects are sufficiently aware of the home builder's construction problems to provide superior design within the realistic framework of the builder's cost and pricing structure.

Yet the market is changing. All industries seek to meet the demands of the consumer, and in housing the consumer is becoming better informed and more demanding.

Almost 40 percent of all new single-family housing is custom contract or owner-built housing. In this category the consumer is entitled to make all decisions regarding design, kinds of materials, and even the specification of individual brands if he so desires. Even most of today's single-family "builder" housing, approximately 60 percent of the market, is sold from model homes, where in order to make the sale more quickly, many builders will permit the buyer a wide range of "optional choices." Different kinds of products, sometimes different brands, variations in the plan of the house, and even the alteration of styling is often granted the buyer who asks. The second-time buyers' market is more a buyers' market than a sellers' market, a fact that has permitted many new homeowners to purchase builder or speculative housing which has been "customized" to meet individual tastes.

Housing, one of America's most important industries, is also the most decentralized major industry in the land. Unlike the automotive industry, it has no Detroit headquarters, no multimillion-dollar advertising budget to promote its new features. Because of the localized nature of the industry and the less effective structure of communications with the American public, perhaps no other major purchase is as undersold or misunderstood.

Communication with the public is an important objective of any industry, and yet because of its multifaced, diverse nature, the housing industry has a huge job before it to accomplish this end. A new house as assembled today represents the combined efforts of many tradesmen, from electrician and plumber to tile-setter and roofing contractor. In many areas each trade is controlled by separate, sometimes conflicting unions. Whether union or nonunion labor is employed, the work is usually subject to a great variety of local building codes, often archaic, which tends to increase greatly the cost of the finished product.

The builder is the "manufacturer" of the final product. He's the boss, the president of the company. Often he must purchase the land, develop it, organize and schedule the work of his subcontractors or his own "crews," obtain financing under the right terms and at the right time, work with city-planning commissions, consider market strategies, local research, new market trends, and new construction techniques. The list goes on and on. It's a big assignment for local industry, and most builders are localized in the scope of their operation. Is it any wonder that good style and design sometimes fall by the wayside?

The intent of this book, then, is to discuss and illustrate one of the many facets of housing—the very important one of house styling. Style is as important in a house as it is in clothes, a new car, or any product where aesthetics, individuality, and choice are involved. Good style, authentic style, helps to increase the value and appearance of a house and adds to the personal satisfaction and pride of ownership.

Influences on housing styles in America have been many. The New World was settled by Europeans of many nations over a long period of time.

Early Spanish settlers in search of religious converts and gold tended to exploit the natives but later mixed with them, creating a blend of cultures and architecture in those areas of the country under the control of the Spanish.

The English, Dutch, and Swedes depended for their labor on their own hands or indentured servants, and when they mixed, they mixed only with each other—not with the American Indian—thereby creating a blend of architecture closely associated with that of Europe.

The French along the St. Lawrence built hipped-roof houses with round corner towers to recall the châteaux and the country manors of France. The Dutch settlers along the Hudson were famous at the art of brickmaking. Their houses were built with gable ends facing the street, stepped gables with windows grouped in the Dutch manner, and Dutch doors opening in two halves like housing found in Holland today.

The Colonial architecture in eastern America, however, became predominantly English, though it often bore the influence of the Dutch, the Germans, and other nationalities. In other parts of America, as civilization moved westward, the influence and resultant architectures varied greatly.

Five of America's leading authorities on residential architecture have assembled their thoughts on regional housing styles and designs in this volume. The director of the Small Homes Council of the University of Illinois, a hub of leadership in today's housing industry, offers his conclusions on the subject.

Each of the five contributors has prepared a chapter on housing styles in his own area of the country. The many photographs used in each chapter along with the descriptive text will be helpful in identifying both the house and the architectural detailing that often marks the authenticity of the style.

Houses in some areas of the country are much more steeped in tradition, an ancestry of design, than in others. In the chapter "Houses of the South," for example, Henry Norris deals in great detail with the specifics of older house styles in order to explain the derivations of the present day. An avid researcher, he concentrates on the influences on housing in the South exerted by early Georgian, Williamsburg, Greek Revival, and French styles.

Mr. Norris, who has his own firm in Atlanta, is a registered architect in all southern states; in addition he holds a certificate of the National Council of Architectural Registration Boards. His work has been in commercial, industrial, and residential design, and his awards for residential design are numerous. His work has been featured in *Better Homes & Gardens, Good Housekeeping, House and Home,* and other magazines. His firm has many clients among America's foremost builders and does many custom-house designs.

John Anderson is eminently qualified to write on house styles of the Northwest. He is both an architect and an engineer—a combination that works well in the creation of exciting new designs. He is a corporate member of the American Institute of Architects and has served as chairman of its Residential Architecture Committee. He is also a member of many other industry organizations. Located in Bellevue, Washington, his firm has specialized in residential housing for the last fourteen years. Many of his designs have been highly publicized.

Most of Mr. Anderson's chapter is devoted to the new styles of the Northwest and the reasons for their development, with much less attention given to the earlier housing of the Northwest, which has little relationship to the newer styles—styles that often show the influence of the Far East, particularly Japan. In other examples the derivation of the style and design is traced to function and to the availability of materials, such as redwoods, cedar, and varieties of pine which have long been abundant in the Northwest.

How does one adequately explain the organization and activities of Richard Leitch? While his chapter "Houses of the Southwest" speaks for itself, Mr. Leitch and his organization are quite a different thing. The first time I visited him in Newport Beach, California, I arrived just in time to see him off for Tahiti, where his designs of a "planned unit housing development" are under construction. His work takes him from Hawaii in one ocean to the Bahamas in another. His clients are among the largest builders and land developers in America. Furthermore, while Mr. Leitch answers to the title of "Mr. Architect," he con-

siders himself a "topogocrat"—a creative designer who devotes as much
consideration to the alteration of land surface as he does to creating the
physical structure, and then "fits them together so that they make
the same statement." Heading a staff of four architects and two designers and employing the services of many consultants, civil engineers,
landscape architects, structural engineers, and experts in marketing,
geology, soils, and foundations, Mr. Leitch and his firm specialize
in total comprehensive environmental design of residential communities and recreational facilities for home builders, developers, and
corporate landowners. This organization has been the recipient of
many awards for prizewinning houses.

Mr. Leitch and members of his staff were assisted by Calvin C.
Straub, Professor of Architecture at Arizona State University, in the
preparation of the "desert architecture" portion of "Houses of the
Southwest."

John Bloodgood, formerly the building editor of *Better Homes &
Gardens*, now heads his own growing organization. Mr. Bloodgood,
too, has placed heavy emphasis on the historical evolution of styles in
his treatment of house styles of the Midwest. Bloodgood, like Norris,
carries the reader from the past up to the present, yet makes it clear
that in the Midwest many of the outstanding new styles express the
influence of the newer architecture of a Frank Lloyd Wright or a Walter
Gropius, rather than that of the earlier stylings of the region.

Mr. Bloodgood's base of operation is in Des Moines, Iowa, where
he and his staff do work for home builders and custom-house clients
in many cities. They work as design subcontractors to builders with
large development areas, providing design goals, specific design direction, and design accomplishment programs.

The fifth contributor to this book is Herman York, my chief collaborator and helpmate in the book's organization. Without Mr. York's
assistance and inspiration the preparation of this book would have been
most difficult. He has been called the designer of more single-family
homes than any other man in America. An estimated 300,000 families
live in York houses, and 15,000 join the club each year.

Most of Mr. York's clients are builders—over fifty-five at last count.
He contributes regularly to the Associated Press feature "House of the
Week" and holds over forty national awards for house design. Practicing in New York City, he is a member of the A.I.A., is registered in
fifteen states, and is a director of the Research Foundation, National
Association of Home Builders. His chapter deals with the more conservative Northeast, where a strong demand for the traditional in
design still exists. Mr. York provides a fine background of the development of these earlier styles, their reasons for being, and their identify-

ing characteristics. He and I share the conviction that public exposure to a wider variety of styles could quicken the acceptance of adaptable styles from other parts of the country, creating an interchange and bringing about a greater interest in new housing on the part of the American public.

Finally, as editor of this book, I thought it important to include the thoughts of one of the housing industry's most eminent and respected academic authorities, Rudard Jones, director of the Small Homes Council, University of Illinois.

His concluding chapter provides a commentary on the preceding chapters and presents his view of the future in housing. He relates the changes dictated by developing technology, new materials and products, and the changing social mores of the country to the influence these changes may have on house style and design.

The Small Homes Council under Jones's direction provides helpful services and activities of a broad nature to builders, architects, and consumers. It conducts a variety of research projects in construction and design, often in conjunction with other departments of the University of Illinois—architecture, home economics, engineering, sociology, economics—depending on the industry's needs. These research findings then find their outlet in a variety of forms. More than five million copies of easily read booklets on all aspects of housing have been sold in recent years. Short courses for building professionals covering residential construction, mortgage lending, estimating, and design are conducted.

Serving as Research Professor of Architecture on the staff of the university, Rudard Jones holds a B.S. and M.S. in architectural engineering and has published almost one hundred technical papers on various aspects of housing. At present he serves on the board of directors of Building Research Institute.

RICHARD M. BALLINGER

HOUSES OF THE SOUTH

Henry D. Norris

HOUSES
OF THE
SOUTH

With its abundance of seaport towns, the South has kept close ties with England and Europe since Jamestown settlement days, and as architectural styles developed in the Old Country, Southerners followed suit, adding innovations of their own to fit their particular climate and tastes. This makes the South a particularly rich hunting ground for today's American family who wants a home with a flavor of the past but with the convenience and comfort of the present.

My comments on southern architecture represent the viewpoint and interpretation of a modern architect who does not believe in taking the historian's or archaeologist's approach when designing today's homes, but rather in realistically using and adapting *influences* of the past. Overemphasizing authenticity can lead to unnecessary complications. Too exact a reproduction of the early home should be avoided; instead we should try for an adaptation suited to today's living conditions.

The availability of many good architects today means that today's homeowner has the opportunity of getting a better-designed home than the owner in Colonial days. Most of the early homes were de-

The President's House, University of Athens, Athens, Georgia,
is a fine example of the Greek Revival style,
3   sometimes referred to as the typical "Southern Colonial."

signed by carpenter-joiners, not by architects. They copied from books of house plans and interior details printed in England which gave specifications for sizes of rooms, mantelpieces, stairways, moldings, and so on. In adapting these designs to the conditions in America, they simplified them.

Today's architect has access to these early books for reference in classical proportions and ornamentation, but his intensive training in design makes him more than a copyist, enabling him to originate details that blend the best of the past with the best of the present. He is better able to visualize the whole building and thus proportion its parts more appropriately.

Any traditionally styled house adapted from the Old South will probably be good, providing the symmetry and detail are appropriate to the particular style. If a house is planned symmetrically, a good architect can design the exterior utilizing almost any style preferred—Greek Revival, French, or Georgian, for example (Figs. 1 and 2). If a floor plan has good interior symmetry but the wrong exterior style, an architect can probably change the exterior to the style desired.

It it quite possible to produce a respectable home today in any of the traditional styles using stock parts. Made-to-order parts are not necessary to achieve an aesthetically pleasing and authentic appearance. For example, traditional molding designs of two hundred years ago are now being reproduced with machine tools instead of hand tools. In many ways they are better and more precise. Many lumber and millwork companies have researched early architecture for their stock mantel designs, moldings, stairway parts, doorway pediments, and the like. It is not true, however, that every company has good designs.

Windows are also a key to authenticity in traditional houses. In the original designs they were narrower than standard windows of today and usually much higher than their width, giving a definite vertical feeling. A commonly used width was thirty-two inches. Joining two windows in a single opening to save money, as we do today, was rarely done. If two windows were needed for light, they were placed separately. Windows extending down almost to the floor were common in the South, because summers were hot and the air closest to the ground is cooler.

Roof lines also help set the flavor of traditional homes. In Greek Revival, roofs were generally lower in pitch than in Georgian and Williamsburg styles, which were quite steep. Roofs in the Greek Revival style, however, were not so important as in other styles. The designers often tried to hide them with parapet walls or very low roof pitches.

Before discussing the major southern styles that influence today's homes, let's first do away with the term "Colonial," used as an architectural style. There is no style as such. Technically speaking, "Colonial" can apply to any building built in America before the Revolution. The same applies to the term "Early American," used synonymously with "Colonial" in architectural context. Neither of these terms really defines a style of architecture. They do become meaningful, however, with an adjective added, such as Williamsburg Colonial or New England Colonial. Even the frequently used term "Southern Colonial" is not definitive because of the many styles of architecture in the South in earlier days. Actually the term "Greek Revival" is more accurate when used to describe the white-columned plantation homes that most of us think of as the typical Southern Colonial home.

This also holds true for the terms "contemporary" and "modern." Many people ask about the difference in these "styles," but when describing a building, these terms do not define different styles; they mean the same thing and can be used to describe any building *not* designed in a traditional style.

The principal styles that influence houses built today in the South, in order of popularity, are Greek Revival, Georgian or Federalist, and Williamsburg (Figs. 3–5). All three styles will be discussed in this chapter, along with French-influence styling and contemporary design.

Greek Revival

The Greek Revival style stemmed from the renewed interest of eighteenth-century England in classical Greek and Roman literature and art—the Elgin marbles, the Greek tragedies and philosophy, and the later Roman adaptations. This contemplative interest moved into the architecture of the day and made its way to the New World about 1830.

The following signals indicate the influence on housing styles of Greek Revival:

1. Use of classical columns with Greco-Roman pediments and cornice treatments, either free-standing or against the wall (pilasters, half columns) (Fig. 6).

2. Use of Greco-Roman ornamental details, such as frets, the acanthus leaf, and shell designs (Fig. 7).

3. Symmetrical plan—often with center hall from front to back (Fig. 8).

Remember that the Greeks originated the simple classical designs used in architecture for columns, pediments and ornaments, leaves, fluting, and the like. The Romans—although their conquerors—adopted the culture of the Greeks.

Symmetry is a particularly important characteristic of the Greek Revival style, and proportions, both correct and harmonious, must be considered in planning each part of the house in relation to the other. In designing traditional homes, the architect must exercise a fine sense of proportion, and in designing Greek Revival homes, he must also have an understanding of Greco-Roman design—its symmetry as well as its fine proportions.

Changing the proportions of the early Greek Revival home to those of modern adaptation is the major pitfall in the use of this style today. Scaling down basic proportions of height to width can radically alter the appearance of any house; in Greek Revival the change is even more extreme.

The height of interior ceilings is the key factor in overall proportions, especially for the exterior of the home. We need to remember that ten-foot ceilings were the minimum in the old homes, and they often rose to twelve or fourteen feet. The early homes, however, were not so large in overall size as we imagine. Therefore, scaling down the twelve-foot ceilings of an old house to the eight-foot ceilings of most modern houses of today understandably throws exterior proportions out of kilter.

The important consideration is exterior proportions. The appearance of interior heights is much less important in modern-day design of this style.

The good architect will use construction tricks to give an illusion of height. For instance, in an early Greek Revival home with a porch, pediment, and four columns, the floor of the porch would have been at the same level as the floor of the house, and the roof line of the porch the same as the main roof. Since the ceilings were high, tall columns were required. Today, we keep the tall columns without the high ceilings by dropping the floor of the porch to the ground line and raising the roof line of the porch above the main roof line (Figs. 9 and 10). This gives the front of the house more authentic proportions that make the difference between a good modern adaptation and a mediocre one.

Another way to give visual height is for the architect to specify that the roof line be several feet above the normal ceiling line, or rather than having the ceiling joists and roof rafters rest on the wall at the same point as is usually done, the roof rafters bear on top of the ceiling joists, thus gaining ten to twelve inches in exterior wall height (Figs. 11–13).

Georgian Influence

Another traditional southern style of architecture being adapted to homes throughout the country today is commonly called Georgian. In the strictest architectural sense the style could well be labeled Federalist or Regency because it came to the eastern seaboard colonies in the middle to latter part of the eighteenth century and carried over to 1830 or so when Greek Revival took over in popularity.

The Georgian style is based on early Roman architectural influences then having a renaissance in England. The southern seaport cities of Annapolis and Alexandria along with nearby Washington and the Deep South cities of Charleston and Savannah found the imposing doorways, interesting windows, elaborate cornices, and fine brickwork of the Georgian house particularly suited to their small but handsome town houses, and the same characteristics can be adapted to individual family residences today (Fig. 14).

Many of the Georgian homes in the Washington complex and in Savannah were row houses, in that they shared common walls and had similar façades. They varied their entranceways and window treatments enough to keep their individuality, and yet there was a pleasant repetition of the general Georgian elements (Fig. 15).

Most of the Washington-area homes were made of handmade red bricks while many of the Savannah versions used stucco, scored into blocks to simulate stone. Savannah homes later used their distinctive gray-brown bricks called Savannah grays.

Charleston homes had a different flavor entirely, often using clapboard rather than brick because of the abundance of wood in the area and adding a West Indian Colonial influence in their long side porches (piazzas or verandas) enclosed with louvered blinds and opening onto side gardens. Though they were close together, the Charleston houses looked more like individual dwellings than their counterparts in Washington or Savannah.

The handsome Georgian entrance doorway of a Charleston home often opened onto the garden rather than onto the house proper. Lacy ironwork was used on gateways and porches in both Charleston and neighboring Savannah (Fig. 16).

Each area had its own variations of Georgian, differing according to climate, building materials available, and local tastes. However, almost all Georgian town houses had some general characteristics that can be adapted to today's home:

1. Bricks. As the chief building material, usually red and handmade, with the exceptions noted above. The bricks were sometimes

laid in the large-and-small pattern of Flemish bond. Quoins were often used for corner trim.

2. Quoins. Projecting stones or blocks of bricks set into the brick-work on the corners of a building for a decoration.

3. Imposing doorways (Fig. 17). Usually raised at least a few steps and sometimes more when a high basement was desired. Since the southern versions were in low-country port cities, the raised portico as a standard element was the result of raising the main living floor for better ventilation and insurance against flooding. Door frames and pediments were often elaborately carved in contrast to the plain Williamsburg doorways. Sidelights and fanlights added more decoration.

4. Front and outside stairways (Fig. 18). Often curving, sometimes double, and as symmetrical as space allowed. Steps were often of marble, limestone, or brownstone.

5. Pediments. Over entranceways, often trimmed with dentils or modillions or both in combination with other moldings. They were based on Roman designs and were more elaborate than in the Greek Revival homes. Roman columns or pilasters were also used in either simple porticoes or more elaborate porch designs.

6. Fanlights. Designed in variations with shaped and often leaded glass panes. In Savannah and Charleston they were sometimes backed by fan-shaped blinds.

7. Double doorways. Not uncommon, with each door narrower than the standard door of today; so narrow, in fact, that both doors had to be opened for easy passage. Brass hardware was often a decorative detail as well.

8. Dormer windows (Fig. 19). With handsome ornamentation such as pilasters, pediments, or curved moldings.

9. Palladian windows (Figs. 20 and 21). Used either at the top of interior stairways or on the façade over entranceways.

10. Lintels (Fig. 22). Over windows, supporting the brickwork, often made of stone or wood designed to simulate stone, sometimes ornamented with a keystone or with frets or rosettes at each end.

11. Roofing. Often slate.

12. Stairways (Fig. 23). Often excitingly dramatic.

Williamsburg Influence

Again, it should be emphasized that the characteristics of any style presented in this chapter provide only a partial definition. Only those elements in modern-day adaptations will be discussed. The objective is to obtain a better understanding of the flavor of a particular style, not its complete authenticity.

The original Williamsburg houses are simple in size and proportions. With a definite English feeling, related slightly to Georgian but more directly to the English country cottage, there can be little doubt of their heritage.

These houses were often the second homes of Virginia legislators and government officials who used them while on business in the capital. Later, however, they were owned by local tradesmen. For these reasons, they were usually small homes on small town lots, not row houses, but individual dwellings.

There were a few large homes in Williamsburg, such as the Governor's Palace and other public buildings, but they were rare, extremely elaborate, and expensive. Unless budgets are unlimited, Williamsburg is not a good style to adapt to a large house. When building this style, the house should be kept small and simple in design, both outside and inside.

The proportions of a Williamsburg house are easy to identify from a photograph because wood sidings and bricks were standard in size and easy to count. Sidings were almost invariably six inches wide and bricks three inches high by eight inches long.

The Williamsburg house is either one and a half stories or two stories, each with its own characteristics. The one-and-a-half story building usually had:

1. Wood siding (Fig. 24). Usually shaped at the bottom into a "half-round" for an attractive finish. The siding was usually painted white or light tan.

2. A steep-pitched roof of wood shingles (Fig. 25). The corners of the shingles were often shaped or rounded off on the bottom edge. Since this is expensive to reproduce today, simulated shingle roofing is often substituted.

3. Dormer windows (Fig. 26). In the steep roofs, to light the small rooms on the upper level. The Williamsburg house often had more dormers, spaced closer together than homes built in other areas of the colonies.

4. Shutters (Fig. 27). More often in a raised-panel design than louvered. Usually dark green, but also dark dull red or dark brown.

5. Windows (Fig. 30). Narrower and taller than are typical today. In contrast to today's practice of aligning the tops of the windows with the top of the doors, they were placed higher on the walls, lined

up with the bottom of the exterior cornice work or top of the door transom.

6. Raised entranceways. Sometimes with a small portico or porch at least five steps up, adding to the vertical exterior appearance that comes with ten-to-eleven-foot ceilings.

The two-story Williamsburg house had these general exterior characteristics:

1. Handmade red brick (Fig. 28). The usual building material, usually laid in Flemish bond.

2. Shutterless windows.

3. Flat brick arches over windows (Fig. 29). Usually of a lighter orange brick than the rest of the house.

4. Roof of medium steepness (Fig. 31). Gambrel roofs were also frequently used to allow more space for rooms than the one-and-a-half story allows.

General exterior characteristics of both one-and-a-half-story and two-story houses were:

1. Fairly elaborate exterior cornices (Fig. 32). Most often using modillions, which are similar to dentils but larger and more widely spaced. Block ornaments, three to four inches wide and spaced twelve to sixteen inches apart, their purpose is to simulate the end of the rafters. They project almost to the edge of the roof overhang. Dentils were more often used on interior cornices. They are the smaller (one and a half inches wide) tooth-shaped trim, usually two to three inches deep, and spaced as closely as three quarters of an inch apart.

2. Windows. Played a more important architectural role than in today's homes. Brick archways were built over the windows on Williamsburg houses built of brick, and wider exterior trim was used around the windows—almost double the width of the two-inch moldings of today. (This is called brick molding.) Greater height gave these windows more importance as well. Wider muntins, the bars that divide the panes, were also used. They were about twice as wide as those of today.

3. Simple, slender porches and wood railing, when used (Fig. 33). Small painted wooden fences were popular, too, not necessarily functional or surrounding the lot but usually as decorative details. Carpenters of the day had fun designing the pickets and posts in imaginative styles.

4. Severely plain doorways (Fig. 34). Usually with six-panel doors and a glass transom above. Exterior trim around the door opening was wider than that used today. Sidelights were rarely used.

5. Multiple chimneys (Fig. 35). With a distinctive shape formed by stepping back the bricks as the chimney ascends so that the top of the chimney is much smaller than the bottom and almost square.

Interiors were quite stark in design but were given interest through decorative wallpapers and painted woodwork that contrasted with the color of the walls. Here are some general interior characteristics:

1. Moldings (Fig. 36). An important decorative detail, usually including a high baseboard, sizable chair rail, and a two-or-more-piece ceiling molding, including at least a flat board against the wall and a crown molding above. Door and window trim was much wider than commonly used today. Moldings were usually painted a fairly strong color, strengthened by adding lampblack, to contrast with whitewashed walls. Authentic Williamsburg paint colors are available from Colonial Williamsburg or local paint dealers. They should be closely adhered to for the proper interior flavor.

2. Wallpapers. Used in hallways, entrance halls, or other small areas. Reproductions of early patterns are available. Again, they were in strong color combinations, often in a floral or bird print design.

3. Paneling (Fig. 37). When used, was of raised-panel design rather than the flat-board style of today. There were few fully paneled rooms. Paneling was often limited to the wainscot (between chair rail and baseboard) or to a fireplace wall and was generally painted except in elaborate buildings like the Governor's Palace.

4. Stair rails (Figs. 38 and 39). Fairly elaborate with a few intricate Chippendale styles. Many of the stock parts available today are too light in scale for authenticity.

5. Light fixtures. Played an important role even in the most modest cottages. Chandeliers, sconces, and wall fixtures were handcrafted of brass or pewter. Several companies make authentic reproductions which can be purchased directly from Williamsburg or through local dealers. It was typical to use a single exterior lantern on one side of the front door in contrast to the pair of lanterns found on more formal styles.

6. Corner fireplaces. Quite common and are adaptable to today's home if planned early enough.

7. Venetian blinds. Made of wood and considered very fashionable and useful by the Williamsburg housewife.

French Influence

The influence of New Orleans on southern and American homes is a different story from other southern traditional styles. Though there was a New Orleans style of architecture (of both French and Spanish origin), the main influence on today's homes comes from families visiting the city and returning home to ask their architect for a "French flavor" in their new home (Fig. 40).

The "New Orleans house" is seldom copied exactly because most were town houses, wall-to-wall, and urban with unique elements based on the city's very hot summers and cold winters. Conversely, most of our homes today are single-family dwellings on individual lots, very unlike the situation in the Vieux Carré. However, there are certain characteristics of some homes built today that tend to give them a French feeling. Few are true adaptations of the typical French cottage or formal French château.

Characteristics that supply a French flavor are:

1. A steep hip roof (Fig. 41). Sloping in four directions rather than two, with very little overhang. The steeper the better for a French accent. Where the house plan is more elaborate than a simple rectangle, for instance having several wings, the façade looks more "French" if the roof line is broken in such a way that the side wings and center core are defined as separate units.

2. Building material. Usually brick, though occasionally of stucco, which is actually more authentic. Bricks are usually lighter in color than English styles: light pink or tan, or painted almost any light color.

3. Windows (Fig. 40). With arched heads and curved top blinds. It is only necessary to arch the brickwork. The windows themselves may have straight tops. The blinds may be painted white, dark green, blue, or even brown.

4. Wood casement windows. Hinged at the sides and opening like doors. More authentic than the up-and-down (double-hung) style. Glass sizes tend to be larger than in the English Colonial styles.

5. Ironwork. Usually cast, on balconies or porches of two-story styles and on front steps and platforms. Wrought iron was used in some early New Orleans homes, but cast-iron designs are a better bet today. Heavier and more ornate, they have a greater French flavor. The New Orleans Vieux Carré homes often had ironwork balconies running around two or three sides of the house; multilevel, they are not very possible or practical today.

6. Quoins (Fig. 40). A detail that adds to the French feeling, used in the same manner as in Georgian homes.

7. Doorways. The double entrance is an authentic touch if the budget allows; again with curved tops and curved panels either in two- or three-panel style on the doors. Size of doors may be wider than in the Georgian house. If there is molding on the door, it should be curved at the top and sometimes at the bottom in a design similar to that seen on French and Italian Provincial furniture. Such doors are available as stock parts and do very well.

8. Interior doors. With straight tops but also with curved molding in a simpler way. Two- or three-panel doors may also be used and are available ready-made. The so-called six-panel Colonial door is better reserved for "English influence" styles.

9. Stair rails. Of wrought iron or cast iron rather than wood.

10. Wood ceilings (Fig. 42). With exposed beams, adding a country French flavor.

11. Mantelpieces. Preferably of marble if budget permits. Otherwise, similar styles are available in wood. They usually project farther into the room than Georgian mantels and often have the edge of the mantel around the fireplace in elaborate curves.

12. Ornamentation. On ceilings and woodwork, if used, deriving its design from natural shapes rather than geometrics; for instance, garlands of flowers or blossoms and leaves would be used rather than the dentils, frets, or classic rosettes of Greek design. Stained interior trim is appropriate in contrast to the trim of other styles, which was most often painted.

Contemporary Design

An interesting story on "What's traditional, What's contemporary?" concerns a European monk of many centuries ago who designed a church, only to have the plan turned down by his superiors. "It is too modern; it has pointed arches, not rounded ones," they reacted. Today his Gothic arches are purest traditional.

To people who ask what style a certain modern house is, we can only answer: "Wait until it's given a name." Someday contemporary architecture may congeal into a formal style and be given a name, but it is not homogeneous enough for that yet. Even the term used, "contemporary," as it applies to residential architecture, is not completely descriptive. Obviously there's a great deal more glass, a more open and spread-out plan, an exterior shape that is noticeably nontraditional and often asymmetrical. But the chief characteristics of the best contemporary architecture are its individuality, variety, and experimentation, which is not true of Williamsburg or Greek Revival architecture, based squarely on conformity and adherence to certain patterns.

A flair for experimentation is needed before "going modern" in new housing because new ideas are the crux of the style. Contemporary or modern styles are influenced by many factors, but two very different schools of thought predominate in influence: the Frank Lloyd Wright school, which stresses the use of natural materials and believes in the integration of the building and its environment, and the International school, originating at the Bauhaus in Germany under the leadership of Walter Gropius. To many Americans, the International Style seems mechanical and severe, whereas to others it is highly functional and its simplicity is especially appealing (Figs. 43 and 44). These schools are quite different, but both are good and appropriate in their design for the American way of life in the late twentieth century.

As for contemporary homes in the South, the trend is toward an informality in design gained by the use of rough, natural materials and a great variety of shapes (Fig. 45). This is in contrast to the Bauhaus style with its flat roofs and severe lines, not often found in the South.

The southern version of "contemporary" is often a compromise of modern lines softened with traditional elements. This stems from the tradition-consciousness of the region and from the fact that building lots are often small and neighbors close (Fig. 46).

A compromise can be found, however, that is satisfying to all concerned—owner and tradition-bound neighbor as well. For example, my own house has a slightly traditional flavor on the exterior, dormer windows, steep-pitched roofs, paned double-hung windows in front— just enough to blend with our traditional neighborhood (Fig. 47). Basically, however, it is a modern structure both inside and out, featuring a twelve-foot sliding glass door instead of a French door in our country French living room, a sliding glass door leading to the patio off the master bedroom, sloping ceilings in the second-floor living bedrooms, and other such features (Fig. 48).

Texture both inside and out is a characteristic of the modern house in the South (Figs. 49 and 50). This is often achieved through the use of natural materials such as stone and stained rough wood. It is not unusual to find some old elements included, particularly things that are handcrafted and a bit primitive. Examples might be a deeply carved Spanish door, wrought-iron lanterns, or a stained-glass panel of simple design.

These traditional elements should be used in moderation, and sparingly. They should be of particularly good quality and styling. It's like a collector displaying a prize piece he found on his travels, but worked indigenously into the house design.

Contemporary architecture brings greater demands both on the architect and on the homeowner's budget. Originality and imagination are required because the architect cannot follow rules and principles from the past. The design process takes more time and is thus more expensive in many cases. The "beautiful clean lines" that go with modern design are hard to come by. Precision is demanded, or the result is shabbiness. Furthermore, suitable stock parts are not readily available; the very individuality of the elements requires that they be custom-made.

"Going modern" can be a traumatic, family-shaking business. One such instance involved a husband who wanted a contemporary house and his wife, who wanted a traditional one. The husband won. After a year of living in a modern-design home, his wife was sold. She "adored" her contemporary home for its ease of maintenance and aesthetic values as well.

Most owners of a contemporary home find it has many satisfactions in addition to the basic one of being more functional. The surprise element is one. Upon entering a modern house, it is impossible to predict what a cornice or trim will look like, whether a ceiling will be flat or vaulted, whether a wall will be of plaster or stone.

In every way, it is usually more expensive to go modern in a new home, but the satisfactions of owning and living in a contemporary residence make it worth the difference for the family not emotionally tied to the past and not afraid to be different.

Captions and illustrations 51 to 61 in this section further explain adaptations of traditional styles in modern-day southern houses.

1. A modern-day Greek Revival, symmetrical in all details.

2. A modern-day example of French-influence styling.

3. A fine example of Greek Revival in the Piedmont area of
Georgia.

4. A Georgian or Federalist house of the South.

5. Williamsburg styling. An example of a two-story Williamsburg Colonial.

6. Classical columns with Greco-Roman pediments and cornice treatments.

20

7. Greco-Roman detail: the acanthus leaf, shell designs, and
    frets.

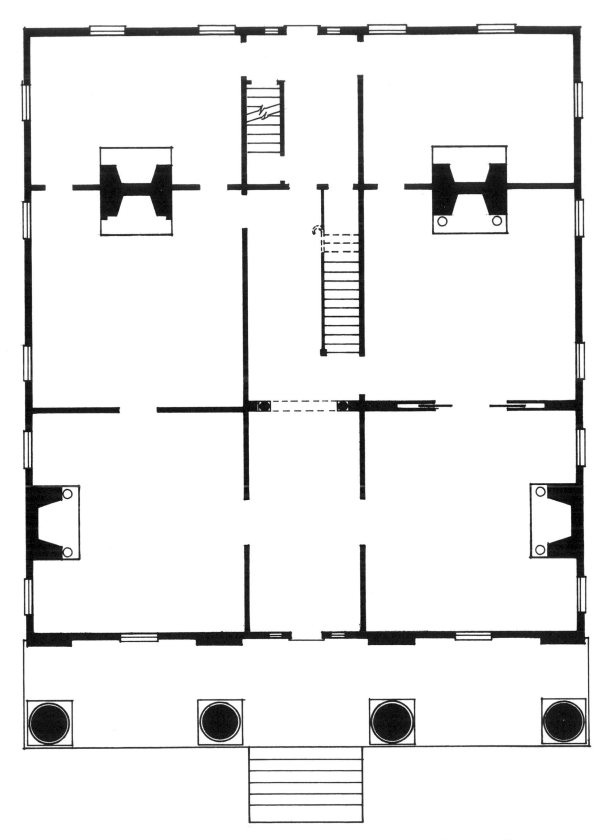

8. Symmetrical plan of a Greek Revival style house. Center
hall running front to back.

9.   Modern-day Greek Revival adaptation. Note the dropped porch barely above ground level permitting use of columns in proper proportion with the rest of the house.

10.   A good example of the modern-day adaptation of the Greek Revival house.

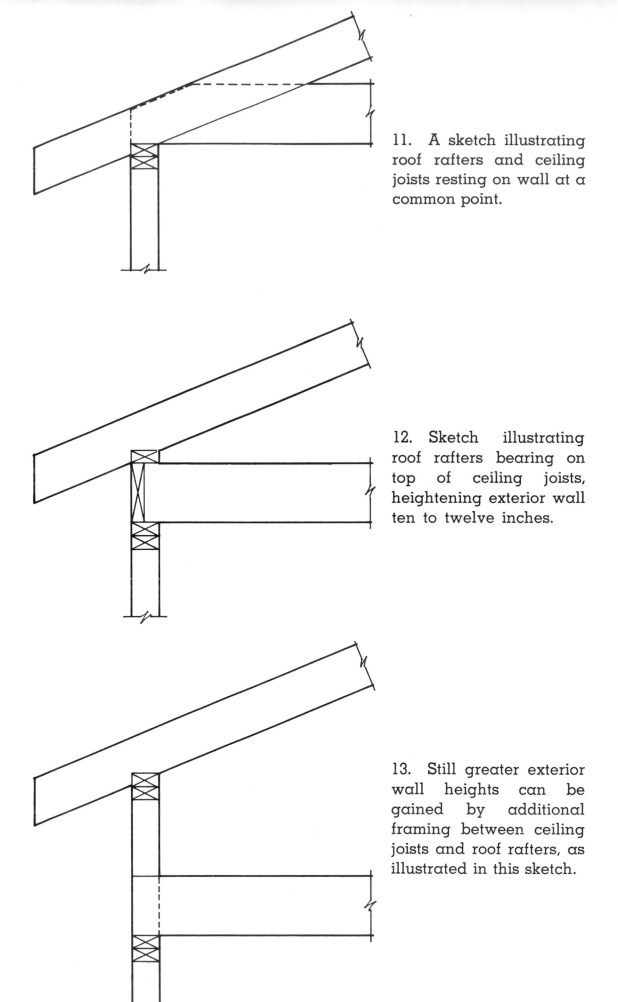

11. A sketch illustrating roof rafters and ceiling joists resting on wall at a common point.

12. Sketch illustrating roof rafters bearing on top of ceiling joists, heightening exterior wall ten to twelve inches.

13. Still greater exterior wall heights can be gained by additional framing between ceiling joists and roof rafters, as illustrated in this sketch.

24

14. A small Georgian town house. Note elaborate detail around doorway, windows, and roof cornice.

15. Georgian row houses with varied architectural detailing.

16. Typical of the fine, delicately scaled Georgian entrances of Charleston. Note the use of flush wood boards with a slightly rough texture.

17. Georgian doorways were raised a few steps, illustrated here, as a means of guarding against flooding in seacoast towns.

18. A symmetrical double stairway, raised sufficiently high to provide better ventilation as well as protection against floods.

19. A dormer window flanked by pilasters and topped with curved moldings.

20. A Palladian window as shown at the top of a stairway.

21. A Palladian window shown as an entranceway from a second-floor porch or balcony.

22. The function of a lintel, as shown, is to support the weight above.

23. Georgian ornamented moldings with a typical partially-
free-standing curved stair.

24. Cross section of typical wood siding used in one-and-a-half-story Williamsburg house.

25. A steep-pitched roof on a story-and-a-half Williamsburg. Shingle corners rounded off on bottom edge.

26. Dormer windows in Williamsburg Colonial are often spaced more closely together than other styles.

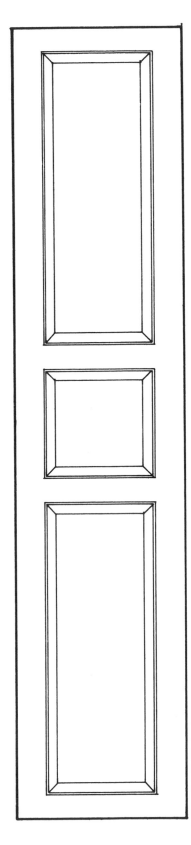

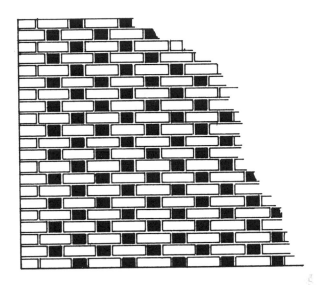

28. Handmade red brick found in the usual two-story Williamsburg.

27. (Left) Raised-panel-design shutters of Williamsburg story-and-a-half house.

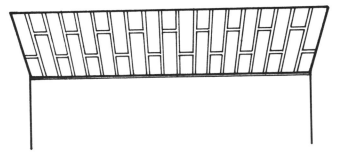

29. Brick arches found over windows of two-story Williamsburg.

30. Williamsburg windows are taller and more narrow than most windows in use today.

31. Gambrel roofs allow more space and are found on many
two-story Williamsburg houses.

32. Both two-story and story-and-a-half Williamsburg often feature elaborate exterior cornices. The modillions shown here are similar to dentils but larger and more widely spaced.

33. A type of porch with wood railing found in both two-story and story-and-a-half Williamsburg.

34. Plain Williamsburg doorway found in two-story and story-
and-a-half houses.

35. The Williamsburg style carries multiple chimneys often with distinctive shapes.

36. Note the high baseboard, the chair rail, and the use of moldings as decorative detail.

37. Raised-panel designs found in some Williamsburg interiors.

38.   Williamsburg stair rail.

39. Chippendale style stair rail sometimes found in Williamsburg houses.

40. A French-influence style of housing found frequently in the South.

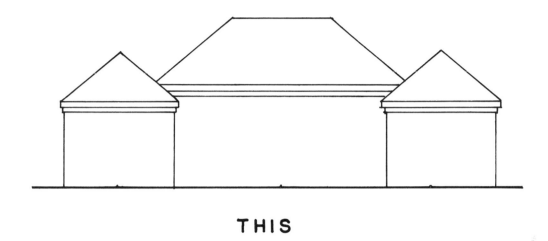

THIS

41. Steep hip roofs covering several wings
of the house can supply a French flavor.

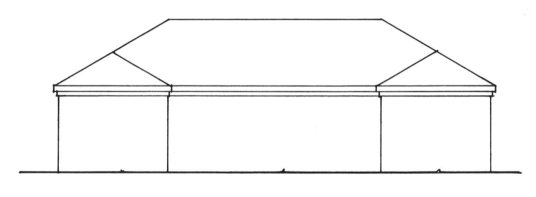

RATHER THAN THIS

42. Wood ceiling with exposed beams adds a country French touch.

43. Symbolic of the International Style under the leadership of
Walter Gropius.

44. One of Frank Lloyd Wright's most publicized houses.

45.   A contemporary house in the South utilizing rough, natural materials of the area.

46.   A southern contemporary house blending modern lines with traditional elements.

47.   The Henry D. Norris residence in Atlanta, a blend of modern and traditional.

48. Master bedroom of the Norris home, again combining the
modern with the traditional.

49.   A modern house designed by Henry Norris.

50.   From the roof deck looking toward the interiors. Figures 49
and 50 illustrate texture as a chief characteristic of a contemporary or modern house of the South.

51. A Greek Revival influence. Note that eave line on center section is higher than side wings; the pediment porch is even higher and the floor line is raised from the ground permitting use of tall columns.

52. Georgian influence. Indicated by entrance treatment.

53. French influence. Note arched head to windows, higher eaves on center part, and twin chimneys.

54. French influence. Steep-pitch hip roof, second-floor windows interrupting eaves line, and curved moldings on front door.

55. Colonial Williamsburg influence. Wood siding. Multinarrow tall dormers.

56. Here the wood siding, steep roof pitch, dormer windows, and typical cornice indicate a modern-day adaptation of the Williamsburg style.

57. Georgian influence. Note the broken pediment trim at front door.

58. Greek Revival influence. Pediment porch with hip roof. Full-length windows on first floor.

59. Mansard roof, curved head on dormers, and double entrance doors indicate the French influence.

60. The style of the house bears the influence of the English Tudor with half-timber construction.

61. Georgian influence. Full brick, ornamental trim at recessed front door.

HOUSES
OF THE
NORTHWEST

John Anderson

HOUSES OF THE NORTHWEST

The Northwest has some of the best residential architecture in the United States. This is probably due to the absence of the traditional and nostalgic influences of the past, which have had a restrictive influence on new design concepts in other areas of the country. The architecture has developed from a natural need for basic shelter and in its evolution has been oriented to the characteristics of the surrounding countryside.

Most of the housing shown in this section was built west of the beautiful snowcapped Cascade Mountains and from the Puget Sound in Washington to the redwoods of Northern California.

The climate of this region is relatively mild in both winter and summer, and although rainfall is frequent, the annual total is not considered high. The country is ruggedly beautiful, providing a glamorous backdrop to a style of housing designed to blend in with nature's surroundings.

The northwestern region of America was pioneered and developed

Extended wood beams, exposed roof decking,
large overhang, and heavy shake roof express the
"woodsy" feeling of Northwest architecture. Heavy log retainers
separate planting areas from the crushed-rock drive.

principally because of its vast timberlands. Thousands and thousands of acres of trees covered the foothills of the Cascade Mountains. The straight and tall Douglas fir, the giant Sequoia redwoods, the West Coast hemlock, and the western cedar were the prime products.

Although there were fishing villages along the seacoast, many of the early settlements that became the cities of today started as saw-mills on the waterfront. Seattle is such a city. Located in part on property given by Indian Chief Sealth, or Seattle, it was the early site of the famed Yesler Mill built by Henry Yesler in 1853. The mill shipped many trainloads of lumber to the East Coast and the central states of America and thus contributed to the growing importance of the town.

As lumber was shipped from the Northwest to eastern United States, it was only natural that many New England carpenters would migrate to this new and thriving source of supply. As they moved with their families to the new land, much of their tradition and culture, including the architecture of the East, was brought along. One of the best remaining examples of this early architecture is the Hasting House at Port Townsend, Washington (Fig. 62). This home was constructed in 1851, a year before the founding of Seattle. Note the fine carpentry detail at the main entry, the window trim, and fascia of this fine old Victorian manor.

Unfortunately, Seattle's great fire of 1889 destroyed most of its early pioneer architecture, and it was many years before a style emerged that was typical of this part of the country. In the intervening years, housing styles were mainly borrowed or copied from other areas.

One of the earliest known examples of an emerging Northwest architectural style which expressed its regional character was created by a young architect, Ellsworth Storey. It was in 1908 that he designed a group of cottages built on the west shore of Lake Washington (Fig. 63). Now some sixty years later they seem quite appropriate in their setting. These structures had generous overhangs, and the stained-wood detailing was both of good design and functional. This was probably the beginning of a new style or trend, yet it was many years before it became popular with the general public. Instead the new families migrating from other parts of the country had their "day in court," and the new housing of the times was nothing more than a replica of that which had been left behind.

This movement of families from the East to the West helps to explain the existence of the many multistyle houses built in earlier days. Also, in more recent years, the Northwest followed the national trends, build-

ing thousands of the typical bungalows of the 1920's, then the
stripped-down conventional stylings of the Depression years, and
finally the simpler lines of the shelter housing of the forties. A housing
style of its own had not yet been claimed by the Northwest.

It was not until after World War II that the Northwest contemporary emerged as a truly regional style. Its development was based
on environmental climatic influences. The mild but frequently cloudy
weather prompted large glass areas without great concern for heat loss
(Fig. 64). The relatively frequent rainfall, combined with the aesthetics
of design, called for a generous roof overhang at eaves and gables.
Again it was only natural that exterior walls should be of native cedar
and redwood.

Although there were a number of Northwest architects developing
this regional style, Van Evera Bailey of Portland, Oregon, and Paul
Kirk (Kirk, Wallace & McKinley), Seattle, Washington, were pioneers in the movement and have provided many fine Northwest
homes of this design.

These post–World War II days, however, found the Northwest
sharing in the plight of a national housing shortage which in turn resulted in the mass production of thousands of small homes mediocre
in plan and design. Not until this shortage of shelter housing subsided
was any general improvement shown. It was only then that new housing reflected the environment of the Northwest on a volume scale and
we finally recognized function as a basic element of home design.

For example, the informal living habits of the people—a function
of a way of life in this part of the country—resulted in the family
room, which was developed for informal entertaining and family living. As time progressed, this room became larger and the living room
smaller. Often the fireplace (a must in the Northwest) was brought
from the living into the family room by design (Fig. 65). Since this
was an informal area, it was logical to use native wood on the walls
and sometimes the ceiling as well (Fig. 66). Exposed structural wood
beams became an integral part of the design (Fig. 67).

More efficient design improved the kitchen. Specific work areas
along with attractive wood cabinets added to efficiency and appearance. Better lighting finally made the kitchen a most pleasant area in
which to work (Figs. 68 and 69).

Centuries ago, when the Cascade Mountain Range was formed by
numerous volcano eruptions, a wide variety of terrain was created.
Much of it is too steep on which to build economically, yet many
square miles of rolling hills were provided on which building with
dramatic effect is now possible.

63

Hills provide a multiple of views from many vantage points and are popular building sites, yet they also present complex construction problems. From a builder's standpoint the hills are obstacles which increase construction costs. To the architect, however, they present a challenge in most effectively orienting design to the site (Fig. 70). The result is multilevels, which can create a more interesting way in which to live. The space relationship from one level to another, connected by an interesting open stairway, is most effective (Fig. 71). Frequently, access from the upper levels is provided to balconies or wood decks as vista areas to the trees and territory around (Fig. 72). In some homes these actually become a design feature of the façade. A number of progressive planning and engineering firms with an awareness of environmental living needs are providing good creative solutions of this sort to housing subdivisions in the Northwest today.

There has also been an appreciable influence derived from the art and architecture of other nations of the Pacific, especially Japan, on the new housing styles of the Northwest. This is due in part to the cultural exchange between the many Pacific seaports, and also to the similar climatic conditions of the coastal regions. In general this influence is represented by a simplicity in design, or conversely, a lack of ornamentation (Fig. 73). The exquisite Japanese landscaping has been an inspiration to many entry and garden courts. The sun decks of the Northwest, as well, have some resemblance to the Japanese *engawa* surrounding many of their homes. Both regions have used wood generously and have placed emphasis on fine architectural detailing (Figs. 74 and 75), and most of the wood is stained in subtle earth tones.

Figures 76–106 feature additional homes which are representative of the new architecture of the region.

62. One of the oldest houses in the Northwest is this well-preserved Victorian house in Port Townsend, Washington. It was built in 1851 shortly before the founding of Seattle. Note the fine carpenter detailing which was characteristic of the period, the paneled entry door, the classic capitals of wood columns, the turned balusters and detailed pediment on entry porch, as well as the window head and sill details.

63. "Storey Cottages," one of the earliest known examples of Northwest regional architecture. Note the good design of simple wood details, the use of multiple sash groupings, relatively large roof overhangs, exposed structural framing, and dark-stained exteriors.

64. This is one of the first post–World War II houses to express the true Northwest contemporary architecture with its wide overhangings and eaves, large glass area extending into the gable set in structural wood, stained "tongue and groove" cedar siding, and heavy hand-split cedar-shake roof. The large roof overhang creates a porch and provides shade for the majority of the glass area.

65. A typical Northwest family room of modest size with a generous fireplace of used brick. The vertical wood paneling and the wood beams in the ceiling help create a warm setting for owners' collection of furnishings. On the left of photograph, family room opens onto a patio deck.

66.   Wood ceiling of tongue and groove extended through glazing of gable to the roof soffit outside.

67. This dramatic interior of multilevel space defined by planes of wood-paneled walls is complimented by the large exposed girder of laminated timber.

68. Modest Northwest contemporary kitchen with oil teak cabinets with "shadow-line" doors. Appliances in brush chrome finish. Partial luminous ceiling. Light panels are used over work surfaces and breakfast area. Ceiling grids are of stained standard redwood sections. Solid ceiling panels are vinyl-covered fiber glass.

69. Contemporary cabinets of oil-finish oak, counters and splash of small mosaic tiles, soft indirect lights for general lighting, and recessed floods over counters for direct working lights. Large dramatic hood with fan and lights suspended from ceiling helps to justify high ceiling. Spice rack in foreground partially screens counter from family eating area.

70. A typically hilly Northwest building site with one of the better design solutions to the rolling terrain. The lower or basement area is open to daylight at grade level. The sun decks on upper level provide convenient outdoor living. The heavy-timber steps make a pleasant transition between levels. The low-pitch roof is built of solid wood decking exposed on the interior. Again we see large glass areas and roof overhangs.

71. Open stair and open risers create an inviting connection for the two levels from the informal entertaining area.

72. Decks and balconies on two levels provide outdoor access from most rooms of the house. This opens the entire house to a sweeping view of Lake Washington, Seattle. Deck balusters are made of 1″ by 2″ stained wood spaced 6″ on-centers.

73. This Northwest house shows a perceptive influence from the architecture of the Pacific Islands. The double-pitch roof slopes and strong vertical lines emphasize the structural elements. The hand-split cedar shakes are indigenous to the Northwest.

74. A close-up of the entry court reveals the rough-sawn red-wood-plywood siding, with vertical cedar battens and detailed corner boards. The vertical detail lines are also carried out on the entry door detail. Landscaping shows influence of the Japanese design.

75.   Entry foyer and stair detail. Floor unpolished terrazzo tiles.
View into living room.

76. Recreation room and bar on lower level. Note open stair detail.

77–78. This home is an excellent example of the very modern Northwest contemporary style. The architect has pleasantly combined the Northwest glazed gable with the modern flat roof. The strong fascia line ties the two roof styles together handsomely. The grouping of the narrow Northwest sash has a modern touch. The glazing in gables is very effective from both inside and outside.

79. A modest house with dramatic lines. The Northwest concept or derivation from the mansard roof has a simple yet pleasing contemporary composition.

80. The cedar shakes weather beautifully and enhance the original texture of the material. The natural stone masonry is a compatible combination of materials. This style is experiencing a ready acceptance and is influencing other building types in the area.

81. The unusual massing of the mansard roof permits this rather high ceiling in the dining and living areas.

82–84. Note structural support assembly for the covered walks from the car shelter to the main house.

85. The house and setting portray the Northwest image well,
and the exposed framing details are consistent.

86. A recently completed fine home with a view of Lake Washington. An outstanding feature of this home is its magnificent wood detail. The exterior illustrates the window and court screening. Note the use of clerestory windows for dramatic lighting effects.

88.   This house is of a Northwest contemporary style having narrow horizontal beveled cedar siding contrasted with the narrow vertical windows of amber glass. The garage was detached from the house structure to preserve a large natural knoll.

87.   (Left) The interior details are exceptionally sensitive, especially the refined details of the stair and balustrade assembly. The large space is warmed by the natural wood paneling and the exposed wood structural members.

89. On the east side of the house are many levels of decks and balconies accessible from all rooms on that side.

90. Virtually all bedrooms are oriented toward the lake and mountains. The sleeping areas are on all three levels of the house, with the parents' bedroom on the uppermost level, which has the most commanding view.

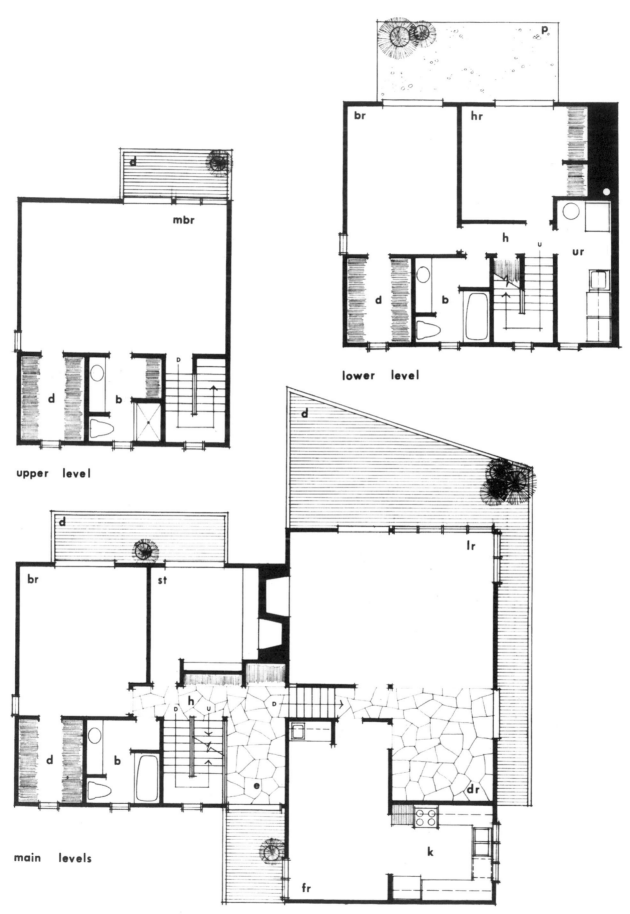

91. Plan of this house, showing upper, main, and lower levels.

92. The one-and-a-half-story-high ceiling and gable glazing enhance the special feeling of the living room . . .

93.   . . . and the dining area.

94.   The interior reflects the same natural feeling as the exterior in the use of resawn cedar paneling as an accent wall in the bathroom.

95

95. The kitchen is elegant in its simplicity. Small yet ample and efficient. Oil-finish oak cabinets with flush doors. Counters and backsplash are of mosaic tile.

96. Here is the Northwest version of the one-and-a-half story of the past. This interesting structure provides space on the second level for two extra bedrooms and bath. Roof lines are enhanced by heavy-textured cedar.

97. This house might be referred to as a classic Northwest style. It has retained the roof lines of the Northwest, but they are carried out in modern masonry.

98. Structural elements are exposed brick columns and bearing walls.

99. Materials are consistent through the entry of exposed brick
with a sculptured brick panel mural.

100. The lighting sets the mood here in the livnig room and library. The detailed beams of the high ceilings are complimented by the continuous indirect light source at the cover.

101. The recreation room is highlighted by the dramatic combination of native basalt stone and a panel of metallic glazed mosaic tile.

100

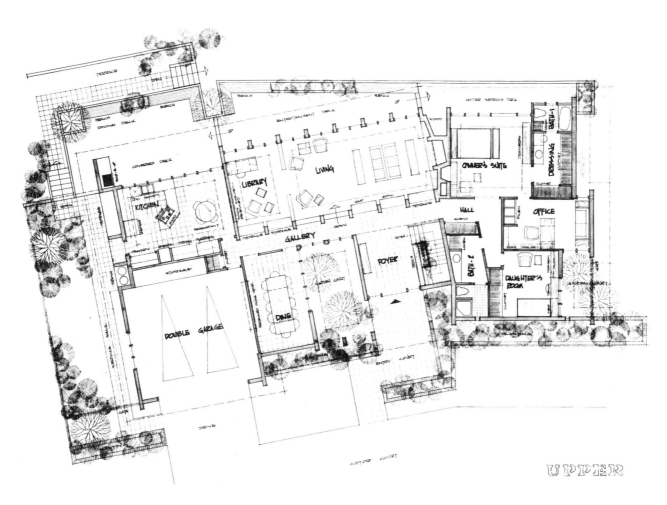

102. Plan of first floor for orientation.

103–105. The mountains of the Northwest draw many visitors who ski in the winter and fish and hike in the summer. Consequently many year-round vacation homes or lodges have been built. This is one of the more unique and unusual structures of the type.

106.   Another striking example of the year-round vacation home
of the Northwest.

HOUSES
OF THE
SOUTHWEST

Richard R. Leitch

HOUSES OF THE SOUTHWEST

Architecture in the southwest region of America has yet to achieve a pure design form of its own. The region is comparatively young, and with the continuing influx of people from all over America, it may well be in a changing state of design requirement for some time to come. Change is typical of the Southwest. Its population is mobile and has been throughout history. A changing people and their cultures have undoubtedly provided the major influence on the architecture of the Southwest.

In New Mexico and Arizona the mixture of the Spanish-Mexican-Indian civilizations created a lasting architecture which has left its mark throughout the Southwest. The Indians in Arizona and New Mexico first developed a practical architecture ages before the arrival of the Spanish. The Pueblo at Taos, New Mexico, is an example of the wonderful towns and buildings these people built with adobe, stone, and wood.

The Spaniards, arriving from Mexico in the eighteenth century, found these structures perfect for the climate and way of life to which they were accustomed. Baroque, the prevailing style in both Spain

Mission-style architecture can be adapted to modern tastes.

and Mexico, was adapted to these simple designs of the Indians, creating a rich style and form of native architecture, best represented by the missions of California and Arizona.

Years after the influx of the Spaniards and directly following the Civil War, thousands of settlers went West, searching for the higher wages then paid in California and the chance to buy land at low prices. These families and the families that followed brought with them memories of the house styles and design forms in the part of the land they had formerly called home. Many influences were then brought to bear on the architecture of these times.

"Monterey" architecture in California, for example, came about when Yankee whalers from New England melded their ideas to the old Spanish "forms" they found in the new country of the West.

Traders from the Far East brought in furniture and materials that began a "Pacific" influence and resulted in an entirely different architecture—a new style.

Early settlers from the East brought with them the clean-cut wood houses of New England and later the influence of nineteenth-century Victorian architecture. Out of this evolved the western ranch house, still a mainstay of western style and a style that has greatly influenced design forms in all parts of the country.

Toward the end of the nineteenth century, several architects migrated to this "Young California" bringing with them ideas of a more "modern" architecture. In San Francisco, Bernard Maybeck began building a new kind of house, the first of the "Bay Region style," wooden and very practical.

In Pasadena, two architects, Greene and Greene, were building great new houses unlike any seen before. Influenced by a combination of ideas from the East and blended with a respect for both Japanese architecture and the basic ranch house already found in the area, they evolved a style that has remained a major influence in the West.

In San Diego, Irving Gill began building mission-influenced modern houses built of concrete and incorporating advanced technology ideas.

These men were among the leaders in developing the new western house styles of today, and all were active before 1918.

After World War I other influences were felt. Modern architects from Europe, including Richard Neutra and Rudolph Schindler, brought with them exciting new concepts. The modern or contemporary style of design was born to the West. Although popular at the time, this International Style of architecture was set apart from the evolution of the western house styles as we know them today.

During this same period the trend toward eclectic design developed as well. Styles from all over the world became popular—Egyptian, English, French, or any combination thereof. Larger houses in Southern California were influenced by the variety of styles on the Italian and French Riviera, and in the 1930's, the Mediterranean style of "stucco porticoes," flat and tile roofs, atriums, high ceilings, and decorative tile became predominant in large and small residences alike.

During the 1940's the trend toward the ranch house outpaced the Mediterranean, and whole communities were architecturally limited to shake or shingle roofs, wood or adobe walls, and a specific roof pitch. These restrictions were well accepted at the time because the style was so universally popular.

Not until the early 1950's did public pressure begin to break these restrictions and permit the use of new materials, varied roof forms, and unusual exteriors. Pacific style, an adaptation of Japanese and Hawaiian architecture, became popular once again.

In Arizona and New Mexico, today as in the beginning, houses show a greater awareness of the climate. The extremes of a desert climate are a demanding influence on house design, yet living in the desert can be delightful if the architect solves the problem of climate and year-round environmental control.

Masonry walls and columns of concrete block or adobe are the building materials most often used. Frequently they are washed with a stucco finish to protect the surface. Wood is used sparingly and is generally rough-textured and stained for protection from the sun.

Floors are often quarry, tile, or scored concrete, the best and most practical surface in a hot climate. Central patios with cool fountains and green plants provide an oasis from the desert. Roof decks are pleasant in the evening, and porches and ramadas (sheltered slatted-wood terraces) provide cool shade and relief from the flare of the sun and sky. Blank walls usually face the west, and carefully planned overhangs filter the sun to the inside. Generally these homes are simple and most comfortable in an informal sort of way.

Figures 107–156 provide some examples of houses of the Southwest.

107. Mission style architecture is the heritage of the Southwest. Since the early Indians and missionaries stacked sunbaked mud bricks to build shelter, the characteristics have been the same: rough-plastered adobe-brick walls, heavy-timbered ceilings, Spanish tile or red brick floors, wrought-iron gates and fixtures, heavy carved doors.

108. El Molino Viejo in Pasadena, California. The adobe home was originally a grist mill and was turned into a residence. It is of plastered stone, brick, and adobe built about 1810 by early American settlers.

109. La Casa de Geromino Lopez in San Francisco, California. A two-story adobe built in 1878 influenced by Victorian and Stick styles of architecture. A meld of two styles.

110.   Built in San Diego in 1856 of locally made brick, this house shows the melding of Greek Revival and Mexican architectural styles.

111. A washed stucco house built in Monterey, California, in 1834 is typical of the style of architecture named after the city.

112. Pacific House in Monterey, California, built in 1835, is an example of Monterey architecture, a combination of Mexican–Spanish–Yankee-whaler architecture.

113. An early *casa* built for Mexicans of sun-dried brick in adobe mortar and plastered.

114. Acoma Pueblo in Acoma, New Mexico, is the oldest continuously occupied village in the United States. Settled in 1540. Two-story pueblos have beam-supported roofs.

115. North elevation of Acoma Pueblo in New Mexico. Plastic adobe brick provides great protection from the heat.

116. An example of an 1851 California Mission style house. Adobe-brick walls, plastered with adobe and whitewashed; roof tiles from San Luis Rey Mission; and an open garden court plan complete with fountain and flowers are among the features.

117. A modern-day design making good use of the Southwest's Spanish heritage. Robert Jones, architect.

118. Another modern design by Robert Jones.

119.   A current-day Pacific style "builder" house.

120.   The Bay Region style of architecture. Bernard Maybeck built the first of this style toward the end of the nineteenth century in the Bay Area of San Francisco.

121.   The Mediterranean style of the 1930's.

122.   William Heuser residence in Phoenix, which harkens back
to Arizona Territorial days. Slumped adobe block makes up major portions of walls and fencing. Wood is used sparingly and
decoratively.

123. Rear elevation of Heuser residence shows patio protected by red-tile roofing, which also shelters living room from hot sun. Tile stairway leads to roof for sunbathing.

124. Residence in Carefree, Arizona, shows adaptation of Mexican villa-type home to Arizona desert.

125. Blank walls "washed" with a stucco finish to protect the surface against the hot sun of Arizona face west on this Scottsdale, Arizona, house designed by Calvin Straub.

126. Columns of masonry and walls of adobe brick are very
often used for desert homes. Windows are fitted with overhangs
to filter the sun, and the ramada, a sheltered slatted-wood terrace, provides cool shade for the patio of this house by Calvin
Straub.

127. Central patio filled with cool fountain and green plants provides an oasis from the hot desert. A slattered-wood roof provides further shade and filter from the sun.

128. High ceiling in living room of desert house aids in cooling.
The early architecture of the Indians, Spanish, and Mexicans
utilized same materials used in this modern-day design.

129. Large expanses of glass can be made to "work" for the
house provided they are given shelter from the direct sun. Here
the huge picture window is protected by the ramada outside.

130.   Very little wood is exposed to the direct sun. Windows are cased directly into the masonry and do not face the bright sun of the west. Washed stucco interior walls and high ceiling provide added feeling of coolness in the house.

131. Kitchen of this desert house has a counter shown in foreground which serves a large family room and a more formal dining room to the right. The floor is of quarry tile.

132. The ranch house, as its name implies, is a product of the wide-open spaces. It is characterized by long, low roof lines, wide overhanging, exposed-beam ceilings, covered porticoes, shake and shingle roofs, massive fireplaces or fire pits, large glass areas, and rustic detailing.

133. The entryway to ranch house shown in Figure 132, notable for its spaciousness. Tile floor and carved doors show Spanish influence on California residential architecture.

134.   From the inside, looking out . . .

135. . . . or from the outside, looking in, this ranch house is a
good example of a house fitted to its environment.

136. A trend throughout the United States is to live in planned communities. They provide an environment of parks, play areas, recreation, and homes instead of the usual rigid lots and fences. The Bluffs, Newport Beach, California, by Richard Leitch and Associates.

137. A pleasant entry to one of the houses in the Bluffs. Note ▶ the Spanish texture stucco, wrought-iron gates, and light fixtures.

138. The contemporary house of the Southwest cannot be put in a mold. This house is an example of the new school of architecture which entered the Western scene in the 1920's, the International Style.

139. A recently constructed contemporary in the Hollywood ▶ Hills area. A dramatic example of the use to which steel, concrete, and glass can be put under the International Style.

140. An example of an all-concrete-and-steel house built in Los Angeles in 1936.

141. Post and beam construction consists of a flat-roofed structure spanning great distances so that no interior bearing walls are necessary. This award-winning home illustrates the open planning made possible by this style of construction. This photograph shows the front entry area.

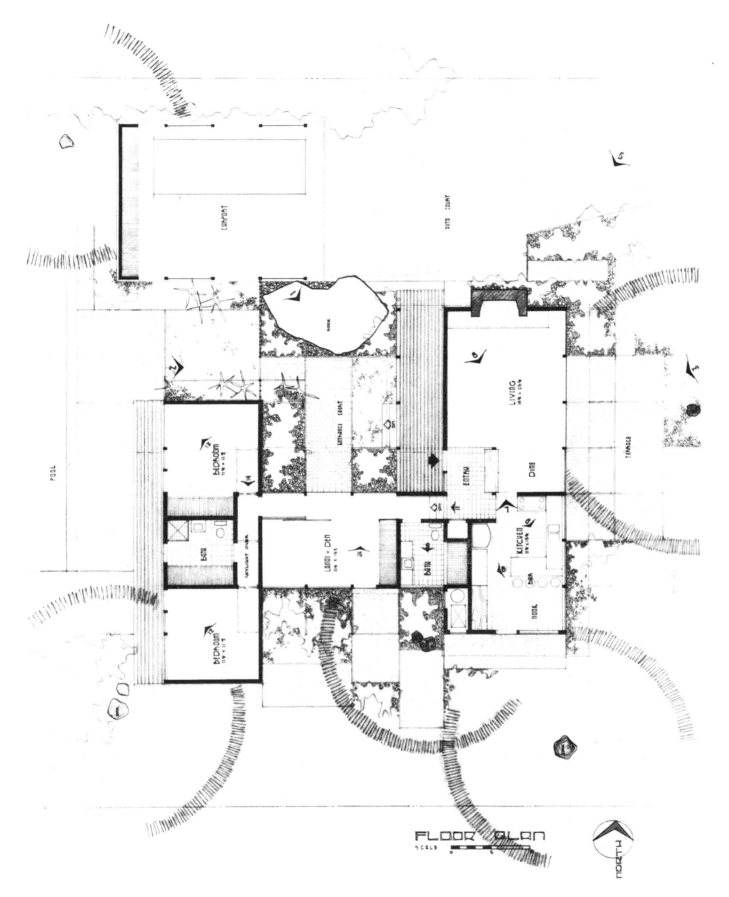

142.   The floor plan, where interior and exterior areas blend in
together as one.

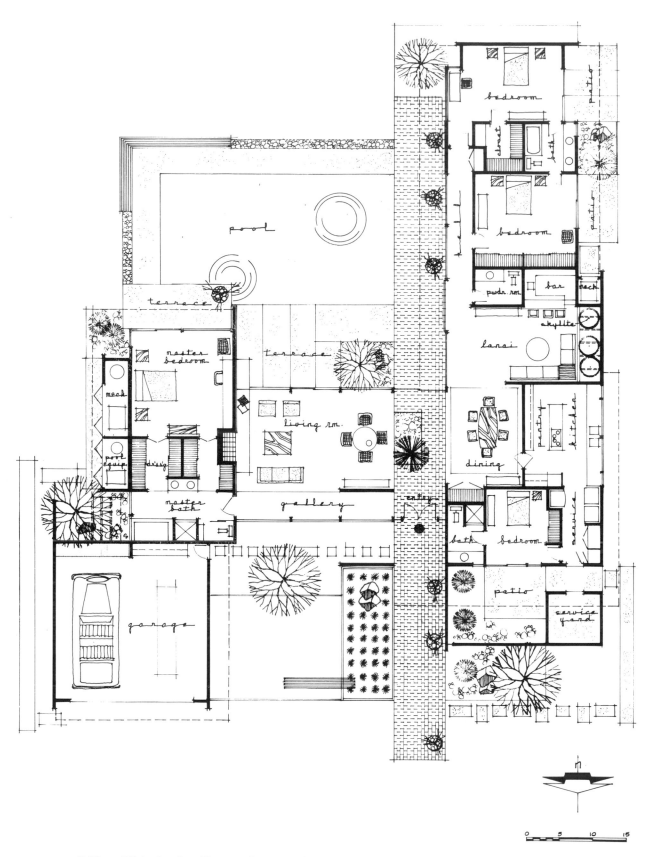

143. This is the floor plan of the house shown on the lead page
of this chapter. The approach is through a long front entry
court. Inside the front door are an entry garden, high ceilings,
and vistas of glass that lead to the terraces and pool area.

144.   This house has been featured as the "Home of the West." Designed by Richard Leitch and Associates, it might be classified as a ranch style, but it is actually a composite of many of the styles so far discussed.

145.   The plan of the "Home of the West" is somewhat open in design. Shake roofs, redwood siding, and exposed rafter ends were used on the exterior similar to the ranch-house style. Mission style influence is apparent in the use of slump-stone masonry and foot-square floor tiles.

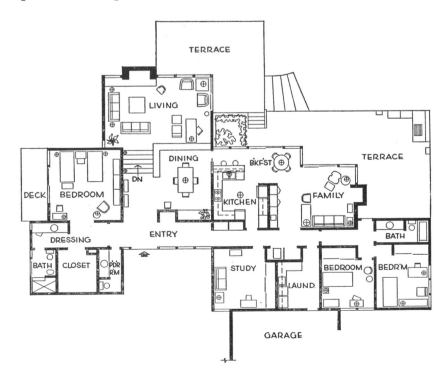

146.　A post and beam type of construction steel house in the desert at Palm Springs, California. It is located on a golf course with the home opened to the view. The floor: handmade tile; the ceiling: flat steel decking; the columns: steel. Note the floor-to-ceiling glass without headers over the doors. William Cody, architect.

147. Another desert house in Palm Springs. Richard Neutra, architect. Wood framing has been used rather than steel, as in Figure 146.

148. Another Neutra house. Again the structure is wood and glass, used with effect.

149.   A covered portico on an adobe house built in Long Beach,
California, in 1844.

150. A modern-day house built in San Juan Capistrano, California, utilizing basically the same red-brick paving and redwood posts and similar *concept* as in house shown in Figure 43, built one hundred years earlier.

151 The home of California architect Gordon Drake. Built in the 1950's, it could just as easily have been built today.

152. An overhead view of the Gordon Drake house, looking down on the patio.

153. Here is an extremely dramatic use of the flat roof, post and beam approach to architecture by Killingsworth, Brady & Smith, architects.

154. New ideas by architects can be strictly experimental, whimsical, or even tongue in cheek, and some are serious attempts from which all can benefit, such as this "tree house" set on a concrete "trunk" with steel "branches."

155.   This is Frank Lloyd Wright's house in the Phoenix desert, constructed of native rock set in concrete walls, with side sunshades of canvas.

156.   This is a house. It is a geodesic dome invented by Buck-
minster Fuller and has many practical applications.

HOUSES OF THE MIDWEST

John D. Bloodgood

HOUSES
OF THE
MIDWEST

The first "housing" units in the early days of the Midwest were log cabins, mud huts, or tepees. By the early 1700's housing as we think of it today had begun to develop. The first owners of these houses were successful merchants whose economic achievements were reflected in their large, proud, and often handsome residential structures which dominated the early settlement towns (Figs. 157 and 158). While the typical dwelling of these times was still the log cabin, the more imposing homes of these early traders and merchants remain to this day as a contribution to the Midwest's architectural history.

These larger, more imposing houses were usually built on the higher grounds surrounding the towns, which were typically located at the junction of two water courses. In a sense they helped to form the first of our early American suburbia, for they were removed from the often dreary, muddy town itself, rather than being a central focus within the town as were earlier eastern houses.

Gradually, as economic prosperity reached town after town in the

The midwestern house of today
expresses a multistyle design heritage.

Midwest, even the average log cabin began to grow into a larger, more accommodating place of residence. In many cases dormers were added to the upper-story loft or sometimes a full second story, and finally the mud and logs were replaced by clapboards (Fig. 159).

The influence of the architect on residential building began to make itself felt in the early 1800's, and styles began to reflect the regional characteristics of their individual taste and the availability of materials. The Industrial Revolution, then in progress, opened up new demands for residential construction, and design development became an objective. As the camera came into widespread use, the inspiring, sometimes monumental, styles of Europe began to be studied and then copied to will.

This eclecticism became the reigning fashion for residential architecture as a result of increasing exposure and the desire to express a new midwestern design culture. Architects copied from the past, added local variations, and a developing architecture of the Midwest began to emerge. These elaborate styles in residential building, heavily influenced by the classical architecture of the Greeks and Romans, spread quickly over the various trading areas, and Mississippi River Gothic and Greek Revival grew up along the rivers and river ports of the region. The intricate metal work of the South and the stone ornamentation so common in Europe were freely translated into the midwestern idiom by use of wooden replicas (Figs. 160 and 161).

During the mid-1800's the population of the greater midwestern area began to swell, and by the beginning of the California gold rush in 1848, fully one tenth of the United States' population lived west of the Mississippi. A strong influence on the housing for these people migrating to the Midwest was Gervase Wheeler's book on "balloon framing" (1855). This provided the building craft a new structural or framing system, and the book was widely used and distributed. The balloon method of framing, a departure from solid walls of masonry or wood, used a timber structural frame with both an exterior covering (wood siding, brick, or stone) and an interior covering (plaster). The quickly adopted system is still the most common residential form of construction today.

One major material development in the Midwest which suited the balloon frame's exterior finish skin was that of mass-produced brick (Fig. 162). Prior to this time, brick was made and baked by hand, used locally and in small quantities. Today, brick is often the basic siding material used in midwestern housing.

At this same period in time, the machine-made nail was developed, and the railroads which were pushing through the territory helped

158

speed up the distribution of this and other new mass-produced building materials. Thus the method of construction from the East Coast through the Midwest became standardized, helping to encourage the beginning of "national styles" such as the Greek Revival, Gothic Revival, Romanesque, and various combinations of these and other eclectic introductions (Fig. 163).

The newly standardized framing system and increasingly available photography led to the publishing of many books on residential architecture, tending even further to unify design interpretation throughout the Midwest. Eventually, developing towns from Ohio to Colorado grew to look alike as the overnight building of hundreds of houses was completed to shelter the onrushing populace. The new technology made no demand on style. It was adaptable to any and every style, since wood was at hand everywhere, was easy to work into ornamental shapes, and was fast to put into position. The first big fashion to be popularized out of these technological developments was the Greek Revival. It spread quickly through the cities and today is the dominant form of the large, older residential structures still standing in the Midwest. Often the true or authentic styles were adapted by the workmen on the job in the smaller towns or cities, or on lesser jobs where no architect was present with his books from which to copy accurately. These somewhat inexact yet prevalent adaptions are known today as Carpenter Gothic and Wooden Greek (Fig. 164).

By the end of the 1870's Greek Revival and Gothic Revival began to lose their appeal, and in their place the Queen Anne style, closely related to the Victorian, became the rage of residential fashion. This new flourishing style was a combination of Romanesque and Gothic, bringing together sharply pitched roofs, towers, stained glass, and balconies. (Figs. 165 and 166). It was a style easy to build and adaptable to a wide variety of housing sizes. It reflected a less formal, more relaxed attitude toward housing; no longer did the Midwest have to prove that it could build palaces in the plains. The Queen Anne style showed less sophisticated restraint and more intricate hand detailing.

Architects to this time had not been working to develop a style more suitable to the new materials and the technology of the day but had busied themselves instead with the correct copying of the old styles or blends of styles to the new vogue. They had ignored the evolving industrial architecture that was being developed to meet the new and broader requirements of the time.

Soon, however, the Midwest was to be the scene of the nation's most important *new* thinking in residential architecture. It was based on the function of a house to meet its occupants' needs. Its development was an outgrowth of the Chicago fire which laid low an entire city just at a time when new capabilities and techniques were proving themselves of great merit in commercial and industrial structures.

The rebuilding of Chicago in 1871 was the first major demonstration of the new emerging architectural style. Architects Louis Sullivan and Frank Lloyd Wright, just beginning to work in the residential field, brought great influence to bear on the entire Midwest. Their Chicago location helped bring many assignments their way in the midst of this great volume of new construction, and the focus of attention naturally turned to both the quantity and the design value of their work.

Sullivan and Wright were both dedicated to their own architectural beliefs and the teaching of these principles to other young architects. Thus their influence spread as their adherents settled in other midwestern cities and developed work of their own, based on the Sullivan-Wright prairie houses. The designs of these houses were long, low, wide, and simple, related to the site, and often quite handsome (Fig. 167). The contrast with the then prevalent Queen Anne and other revival styles was sharp. The people liked the looks of these long houses which better suited the broad vista of the midwestern horizon.

In the early 1900's and until the years following World War I, Chicago was again to play an important role in several residential design trends. The Chicago Fair was a restatement of the grandeur of the more formal early Greek and Roman styles, and revivals of these styles began to spring up once again. And then after World War I the counter-influence of the outstanding modern architects in Germany and Czechoslovakia was brought home from the war to become much discussed and imitated. The modern design of the pavilions and villas of Europe was soon to appear in similar fashion throughout the Plains. Again the Midwest was searching for something better to fall back upon. And in so doing, the Midwest, usually associated with a cultural lag, became the first real testing ground for "contemporary" or "modern" residential design in the United States. During the 1930's many houses still considered modern today were built throughout the Midwest. In this period, as an example, Frank Lloyd Wright built his famous Taliesen at Spring Green, Wisconsin, and students flocked to see the new design principles (Figs. 168 and 169).

Throughout the 1940's and much of the 1950's, while these principles of modern design were being refined and admired, new housing for the majority was copied from the nation's early history. Colonial housing, so prevalent in the East, came into vogue for the first time in the Midwest. The midwestern version was often repetitive of eastern tradition, yet many variations appeared, indicative of regional influences (Figs. 170 and 171).

In these post–World War II days the housing industry was looking for further technological and labor-saving advances. Prefabricated housing (Fig. 172), soon to be called manufactured housing, began to take its first big strides in the Midwest as a major supplier of housing units. These earlier houses were production units providing shelter at the lowest cost possible. They were developed for speed of construction, easy site erection, and greater economies in both volume material purchasing and fabrication. The "manufactured house" industry still thrives in the Midwest and grew to produce larger and more stylish houses than in earlier years. (Figs. 173 and 174).

Finally, the influences of modern architects and the principles of design based on functional living became more and more evident as we moved past the shelter market of the 1940's and the early 1950's and a more affluent second-time buyer came into the marketplace. The ranch house had begun its trek from West to East and on its way was moderated by midwestern influences. Styles changed from the original rough-hewn western ranch house to the brick and asphalt of the Midwest. The change was not in the mass or the low, long proportion but more in the detail and resulting character. The midwestern ranch house attempted to combine the simplicity of modern thought with the freer plan of the western ranch and its scheme for indoor-outdoor living. When it was well done by an architect, it was pleasant enough, though often quite different in character from the more conventional one-story ranch house as we have come to think of it today (Fig. 175). As the ranch house moved farther eastward, it developed the colonialized façade so prevalent in other eastern housing. In both the Midwest and the East, however, the major appeal was in the open, informal way of life the houses allowed.

By the 1950's and early 1960's several of Europe's more prominent architects had settled in Chicago and associated themselves with the modern movement. They began to develop houses of great simplicity and sophisticated beauty. Complete systems of glass walls were designed rather than the fitting of a glass unit into another wall system. Flat roofs expressed more lightly the lines of the earlier Wright prairie house. Ornament was nonexistent; proportion, natural material use, organic siting, and spatial relationships were the important guides to their refined designs. Adherents of the European school of modern architects set their cubistic buildings on platforms above the ground to symbolize man's triumph over nature (Figs. 176 and 177).

These houses were sophisticated in the extreme, yet the current mood of living in the Midwest was becoming more and more informal. The cubistic houses were beautiful to enjoy as architectural sculpture but demanded a discipline of its occupants. The Midwesterner of the period was ready for the aesthetic values and the great feeling of space and the outdoors the design provided, but not the ordered life that the houses demanded. The compromise was to still use the horizontal line, the lighter treatment of planes, the greater use of glass, the natural expression of materials, and the organic siting, but with less formality and ordered design character. The casual overcame the formal, and the houses were relaxed, pleasant, and had great character (Figs. 178 and 179).

Today, design trends continue to develop in the Midwest as they always have. Influences of the East and West coasts are combined with midwestern materials and sites. More and more frequently, for example, do we find West Coast woods sheathing a midwestern ranch plan (Fig. 180).

The midwestern heritage of the early romance of frontier life suggests forms today that are a departure from anything in the past. More and more new housing is fanciful, suggestive of enveloping enclosure while at the same time open and related to the site. Courtyards help define family privacy on the flat terrain. Midwestern brick staunchly surrounds the framework. Glass areas are protected by overhangs and projecting walls. The simplicity and neatness of contemporary planning and design combines well with romantic forms of earlier residential building to bring together the new design philosophy now in evidence (Figs. 181 and 182).

Houses often look like a collection of farm buildings with various roof planes and pitches all leaning toward a central mass. Texture and form become heavier and more defined, giving ornament and character without fussiness. Planes also reflect the double goal of openness with privacy. Main rooms flow together, but visual blocks, carefully placed, give each space an individuality of scale and character (Figs. 183–185).

The relaxed, personal character of midwestern life is expressed in these easygoing design ideas suggesting the more formal styles yet without exact duplication. The massing has a vestige of revivalism, but the overall effect is current and simple. Spaces inside open and close from each other to provide changing proportions and function, basically casual rather than rigidly defined (Figs. 186–189).

157. Borrowed details from eastern colonies made the mid-western houses look somewhat traditional.

158. This Illinois home was typical of the newly successful Midwesterner's search for status.

159. The more typical house of the period was a simple enclosure, with local field-cleared wood siding, small windows,
and basic trim.

160.   Every design ornamentation could be copied in wood, and was. Note the wooden "ironwork" at doors and windows.

161. Greek columns made every house fashionable, no matter
what the style of the basic design.

162.   Brick became a mass-produced commodity and started its
still fashionable vogue in the Midwest.

163. The Illinois Historical Society has been saving excellent examples of these well-executed revival styles.

164.   The Carpenter Gothic and Wooden Greek styles borrowed
freely though not exactly from history.

165. The Queen Anne style in the Midwest added stylistic trimmings to basic revival styles.

166.   Architects developed the Queen Anne style still further to
a high and elaborate art replacing the earlier revival temple designs.

167. Frank Lloyd Wright's famous 1909 prairie style, Chicago's Robie House, used structure and architecture as an organic whole, with long, low lines and cantilevers relating to the wide midwestern horizons.

168. Frank Lloyd Wright's home and studio, Taliesen, in Spring
Green, Wisconsin, used native stone in this 1925 development
of his organic architecture.

169. Structural engineering refinements led to new materials being used for residential construction.

170. "Colonial" trimmings adapted to the boxy midwestern farmhouse style tried to bridge the gap between frontier necessities and eastern culture.

171. As Midwesterners and Easterners became more inbred in business and social relationships, more exact eastern styles found their way into midwestern houses.

172. The "prefabs" of the early development days answered the Midwest's call for inexpensive housing during post-Depression years.

173. After World War II, "prefabs" were dramatically up-
graded and reflected every style, size, and cost range.

174. Manufactured houses, distributed nationally but predominant in the Midwest, often introduce new design ideas into local residential markets.

175. Perkins & Will, architects, combined the "prairie" design feeling with western ranch house character, part of a whole new design trend.

176. Mies van der Rohe gave residential design an extreme of sophistication, structural elegance, and formalism in the Farnsworth House.

177. This 1950 Frank Lloyd Wright house embodied organic design blended with greater material freedom—simple economic midwestern materials.

178. The sophisticated shape of the cubistic house was softened in detail treatment to reflect more relaxed, informal living patterns. Geo. & Fred Keck, architects.

179. The shape of housing began to reflect the more casual in-door-outdoor living of young families.

180. Housing can also reflect the more romantic, fanciful character of prosperous times.

181.   As suburban developments ringed midwestern cities and
towns, privacy became a more important design necessity.

182.   Massing and glass areas alternated more and more often
to give a pleasing combination of openness and enclosure.

183.   The sense of enclosure became more and more important
in residential design development as expressed by architect Ed
Dart's treatment of the midwestern barn.

184.   The grouping of various masses assumed a completely informal character, as if by nature rather than design.

185. Structural elements were more typically exposed to combine staunch warm texture with the sophisticated pattern of supporting design.

186–187. More formal earlier styles were newly expressed in
formal yet still relaxed housing shapes.

188.   The scale and stature of taller proportions gave more dignity to houses during the early 1960's.

189.   The simplicity of interior detail and trim allows great flexibility in accommodating interior design tastes.

HOUSES
OF THE
NORTHEAST

Herman York

HOUSES
OF THE
NORTHEAST

A large proportion of the interested general public is often at a loss to classify much of the new housing being built today. "What's the design?" is a question asked by many prospective buyers of new or existing older housing. This confusion is perhaps more understandable as it relates to newer housing. If the house was built during or before the nineteenth century, identification becomes simple because most of its period characteristics are incorporated in the overall design. Moreover, classifying such a house according to its style category can be made with little risk of error by the informed, since earlier designers gave careful attention to proportion, balance, and detail.

However, when applied to the houses of today, such classification or recognition becomes more difficult. Few twentieth-century homes are complete authentic design copies. They carry many of the elements of early houses, but a mansard roof by itself does not make a French Provincial. Furthermore, today's new home lacks most of the

Showing the front elevation of a house
in New Seabury, Cape Cod, this outstanding design
by Claude Miquelle utilizes sawn-board siding and
cedar-shake roofing in conformity with the natural setting.

fine handcraftmanship that was so closely associated with the predominant styles of yesteryear. The present-day shortage of skilled workmen coupled with high labor costs in the building industry has made these features prohibitive in cost.

In much of the new housing built in the Northeast today, Early American intermixes with modern forms of uncluttered simplicity to produce a crossbreeding of style. To compound the problem of identifying the modern-day house as to its style, many "sales features" are added in an effort to further intrigue prospective buyers. This is more true in mass-produced housing, where it is not unusual to hear such comments from builders as "We must use more brick on the front of the house; buyers want more brick." Thus a reasonably well designed house, authentic in overall character, is diluted quite unknowingly by the builder in his search for additions to the house that create "curb appeal"—the elusive quality that makes prospective buyers stop, look, and then buy from the model-house offering.

In today's market of second-, third-, and fourth-time home buyers, most smart builders believe it necessary to cater to the tastes of the better-informed, better-heeled buyers who want improved quality and more status in their next house. Similarly most buyers are becoming increasingly aware of design as an important quality ingredient in the new house and are as well able to recognize it. This enlightenment on the part of builder and buyer should ultimately result in improved new house design. Not just builders but mortgage lenders and government agencies such as the F.H.A. are giving new house design much more attention.

Another factor influencing house design is the development of new materials. Many of the newer materials are researched and produced on the basis of their use in engineered modular construction, a system utilizing standardized units, or standardized dimensions of components, for more efficient, more economical house construction. Modern design, therefore, is most often the vehicle through which such new components find a market.

In most instances it is inaccurate to label a house built in recent years as Cape Cod or Georgian, etc., the carry-over from earlier periods being evidenced only in its general mass. Many houses built today called Cape Cod resemble the original only in their high-pitched roofs (with space in the attic for additional rooms). Among the many differences the current model may be sheathed in aluminum or steel, manufactured "used" brick, or plastic-coated plywood, chemically treated hardboards, or sculptured concrete block.

A thoroughly misleading classification identified with Cape Cod style is the so-called one-and-a-half-story house. This is a confusing

200

designation, for it is logical to assume that any story that qualifies as a place suited for habitable area must also be accepted as a full story, not as a "half story"—this regardless of roof shape.

There is similar confusion in the use of the word "Colonial." Many Northeasterners use this word as the name for any traditionally designed *two*-story house, thus combining "style" and type of house in a single title. The inaccuracy here is quickly seen when the designation is applied to a two-story house of modern design.

Style and type are totally unrelated. In this volume we deal exclusively with style origins and differences, showing by example the factors that have had the greatest influence on present-day home building design.

Much of style influence in the Northeast can be attributed to the places of origin of the first settlers of the area. Many of these pioneers emigrated from England, France, and Holland. The Spaniards settled in the Southwest, and thus two general areas were formed, one on the Atlantic coast, heavily populated by the British, and another in the Southwest, inhabited by the Spanish.

In the initial stages of gaining a foothold on American soil a crude hut was the symbol of the domestic architecture of the time. Most of the seventeenth century in America was spent in the conquest of new frontiers and the establishment of farming areas, activities that indicated the country's future agricultural and industrial greatness.

In these early years most of the building was done in comparatively safe areas near the coast or along rivers leading back into the virgin timberlands of an unspoiled country. The early settlers, new to the area, were confronted not only with problems involving home construction but also with generally hostile North American Indians. Thus protection from the weather was only one aspect of a building operation. Houses were simple, designed primarily as shelter, reflecting the rugged character of the land and the simple life of the New World.

The climate of the Northeast influenced design, as it does in all areas. Steep-sloped roofs to shed the snow and excessively thick walls to insulate against the cold were common practice. Homes of the Northeast were planned with a greater degree of compactness, with the kitchen as the control center for all the family activity. Usually a huge fireplace dominated the kitchen area, and to conserve heat, ceilings were low and rooms quite small. Windows too were small to minimize heat losses through the glass.

Seventeenth-century houses in the Northeast were varied and lacked design direction. Influences are detected from many areas of Europe. Not until the eighteenth century did Colonial styles come into being, when the rugged character of the 1600's gave way to more sophisticated detail, still essentially done in wood but with greater skill and finer craftmanship. In these houses one sees the influence of entire areas of Europe, which centuries before were affected by the architecture of Greece, Rome, and the Middle East. By the beginning of the nineteenth century the Colonial style had given way to various forms of Georgian, an architecture that in turn by the middle of the nineteenth century had lost much of its stature. A strong but short revival of Greek and Roman styles then took place, but the century closed with the splendor and flamboyance associated with the Victorian era. This low ebb in American taste, particularly in architecture, set the stage for twentieth-century contemporary design.

For varied reasons, however, many of which puzzle the architectural mind, an eclectic movement then developed in which traditional Early American influences were profoundly apparent. The great innovation employed today in the architecture of commercial, educational, and religious buildings has had very little influence on residential design of the Northeast.

The "warmth and charm" of an Early American house, referred to as "heart tug" by an editor of one woman's magazine and praised in many quarters, has placed it in a favorable position with most of what is done under the label "modern." In this part of America newcomers and longtime residents alike have traditionally preferred the earlier designs, the traditional designs, known and accepted by the generations that have gone before, and the for-sale house more often appears to find a ready market when the design is as nearly authentic as possible.

However, a gradual trend toward more reactionary design is apparent. An influencing factor has been the development of those new materials that embody in texture and color the attractiveness of those used in earlier decades.

Architects by training prefer a modern house but have not as a group successfully promoted it because of lack of understanding on their part of problems created by the modern-day science of home building. The innovative design that the architect strives to incorporate in his house very often represents to the builder high construction costs which tend to price his houses out of the marketplace. In the Northeast a departure from conventional methods of construction is perhaps more costly than in other areas. In short, then, houses in the Northeast are more conventional than in most areas and the influence of the architect is less apparent.

Consumer preference for traditional design in the Northeast has further played a major role in resisting the change to modern, reflected in the building codes and ordnances of many localities. Rulings to the effect that "a house may not be built which in appearance is either too similar or too dissimilar to that of its neighboring dwellings" are not uncommon. The intervention of municipal controls over taste, though perhaps warranted in many instances, nevertheless tends to limit the development of innovative design which could play a major role in the development of a stronger architecture of the future. Limitations on choice are often imposed on families of good taste who may prefer certain neighborhoods but not the prevalent styles of housing found there.

Let it simply be said, then, that the laws regulating aesthetics and influencing style go beyond "protection of life and health" and sometimes to the disadvantage of good design and individual expression.

The photographs that follow (Figs. 190–223) give examples of both the earlier traditional houses and the later-day houses whose design the traditional so greatly influence. This latter group is typical of those built during the 1950's and 1960's. They represent for the most part the homes of middle-income residents of the Northeast.

A wide range of styles does not exist in this part of the country, and therefore although "custom housing" is more innovative, the author of this chapter has chosen to show more examples of modern-day "builder" or "model home" or "tract" housing simply because it is more representative of the vast majority of houses being built in the Northeast.

The traditional house of today can claim only a distant relationship to its predecessor. Often the relationship is little more than shuttered windows or walls covered with hand-split shingles. A modern-day traditional, however, need not be authentic in every detail to be well designed. By the same token some of the newer homes pictured will show a closer relationship to modern, employing newer elements of detail yet retaining traditional forms.

The Northeast styles of today could perhaps be classified as a new traditional design that attempts to bridge the chasm between yesterday and today.

190. One of the few surviving examples of a simple and picturesque type of home built by the first settlers in the Pennsylvania German country.

193. Note the three balusters to each tread and the raised paneling on the walls and each stair tread end.

194.   An example of an early nineteenth century Pennsylvania German farmhouse, showing typical facade of the period.

195.   One of the oldest well-preserved examples of a Georgian mansion.

196. A typical cottage of Cape Cod design. The asymmetrical front elevation, off-center chimney, and simple roof line all contribute to make this a symbol of the Cape Cod traditional exterior. Great numbers of such houses were built for the shipbuilders and fishermen in the Massachusetts area. They were minimum houses and so well suited the needs of the people that larger houses were not built until many years later.

197.   One of the oldest houses in Deerfield, Massachusetts. Simplicity is an important ingredient. All windows on both floors are identical in size, contributing to the serenity and beauty of its elevation.

198. John Howard Payne Memorial "Home Sweet Home" illustrates the "salt box" design at its best. Old shingles, beautifully
weathered, add texture to a facade that needs very little to enhance its attractiveness.

199. A well-preserved example of a typical early frame house.
Relationship of wall space to window and door openings shows
appreciation of scale. Additional balance is achieved in part by
locating window heads above top of front door, typical of such
early design.

200. When viewed alone, the details making up the pediment, entablature, and frieze appear heavy, but as an important element of the two-storied facade, the entire doorway is brought into scale.

201. Exterior side view of typical Dutch Colonial gambrel roof.

202. In this eighteenth-century house, first-floor window heads are carried well above the height of the door. The high front wall is achieved by a plate located above the second-floor ceiling creating more third-floor space. Note the typically narrow clapboard siding.

203.   This is a small frame house with Greek Revival detail typical of the 1830's and 1840's.

204. An outstanding example of early Federal architecture which illustrates some of the detail used during this period.

205. With New England influence in much of it, this house is of more recent vintage in such detail as the gable and overhang, the design of the chimney, and the absence of moldings over door and window heads. Design purists will object to such features as grouped windows with nonfunctional shutters.

206. This "all-wood" house is known in homebuilding circles as a farmhouse. It shows very definite influences of the Early American period primarily in the simplicity of the forms that make up the total design.

207.   This house carries a strong late Georgian influence, sometimes called Post-Colonial or Federal. The absence of classic columns and entablature around the front door using instead the standing seam metal roofing adds an element of contemporary design. This is also true of the manner in which quoins are built in of brick in the corners, rather than the usual staggered quoins in white.

208.   This modern-day design carries with it interesting influences of French detail, as evidenced in the arched heads over
garage doors and dormer windows. An interesting design device is the use of the horizontal band of brick at the sill level
carried across the front of the house to line up with both the
cornice of the garage roof and the top of the privacy wall.

209.   Influenced by the Early American version of Cape Cod
and bearing a Dutch gambrel roof, this modest house is beautifully proportioned. Glass proportions of windows in the dormers
match those of lower windows.

210. An updated version of the Cape Cod cottage with the additions of habitable attic rooms. A large chimney adds authenticity to its design. The garage and connecting section are well proportioned to give overall balance. One cannot over-emphasize the simplicity that accompanies most well-designed homes. Here it is quite evident.

211.   This house is beautifully proportioned, using Greek Revival detail in the low-pedimented doorway flanked on each side by simple classic pilasters. Corner pilasters used on the projecting wings of the bedroom and the garage, and the symmetrical exterior, are typical of houses built during the original Greek Revival era.

212. In this new house the entablatures above door and window frames come from the mid-eighteenth-century house. The location of the chimney shows a later influence as well. Earlier houses used a central location for fireplaces. The boldness of the window frame and its entablature eliminates the need for shutters.

213. This modern design represents the maximum in contemporary appearance and detail which speculative builders in the Northeast will offer buyers. A bold white roof contrasts beautifully with the dark stain of the house itself. The long horizontal roof lines combine with the sheer vertical lines of the windows to create a feeling of both spaciousness and simple elegance.

214. The author's own home, which he designed to take advantage of its wooded two-acre setting. The pine siding is of sawn-board finish which retains on the lower edge the actual shape of the tree trunk. The center section utilizes Roman-size ivory-colored brick laid in a stacked bond.

215. Entrance foyer of the York home.

216. Another example of a recent house designed to incorporate simple New England detail in clean, uncluttered planes. The narrow clapboard lends scale and dignity to the elevation which, through its imposing mass, gives adequate visual support to the large chimneys.

217. A fine example of contemporary design with a New England flavor. Built in Cape Cod and designed by architect Claude Miquelle.

218.   Detail showing deck area with simple yet handsome deck
railing of Miquelle house.

219. Private rear patio and deck areas of Miquelle house.

220. An example of how the simplicity of contemporary design can be used to produce attractive wall areas. Here brick, glass, and wood are combined in excellent scale using unpierced walls to provide privacy for interior atrium garden. Irving Saunders, architect.

233

221. View of the atrium garden. The architect carries through to the interior court the character of the exterior by using the same materials and design elements.

222.   Rear elevation of Claude Miquelle house in New Seabury,
Cape Cod. Note the projecting roof ridge over larger section
which provides shading and protection for the upper glass
areas.

223. Rear patio in New Seabury house.

CONCLUSIONS

Rudard A. Jones

CONCLUSIONS

Present-day designers of homes in the United States, in their search for better residential architecture, seem to be pursuing two different philosophies. Those who are more traditionally minded base their work on the successful architecture of the past; architects with a contemporary viewpoint use functionalism as their principle, ignoring historical examples and period styles.

While "style" is often used in reference to tradition-influenced architecture, the "styles" of contemporary, modern designs are not always so identifiable because of their more recent origin or local nature. Obviously, a "style" is not created overnight; it is developed over a long period of time as changing factors influence its evolution.

All good styles in their purest form relate to their early environment and the existing conditions of the times. The building needs, climate, site, available materials, and available skills, tempered by the historical background and objectives of the people concerned, contribute to the development of a style.

Styles are not static. Changes in the availability of materials can vary the style. For example, even though the divided light, double-hung window is considered representative of Colonial architecture, research indicates that the earliest windows were most likely of the casement type and the sash glazed with diamond-shaped panes of glass. As the size and shape of the glass shipped to America changed, the double-hung window became common.

The development of an architectural style is always closely related

The English half-timber house uses
wood framing with spaces filled with masonry.

239

to a particular structural system, but as time passes, the structural basis of the style may be lost and only the external characteristics will remain. The New England house of the pre-Revolutionary period, for example, was framed with heavy timbers that were erected in a fairly standard form. This frame influenced to a considerable degree the final form and appearance of the house. Today's New England Colonial house has much the same form and appearance as its eighteenth-century counterpart, but its construction system is entirely different.

Is it an anachronism, then, to copy or adapt traditional patterns in designing new homes today? The answer to this question depends entirely upon the point of view. Most critics would agree that if the spirit of the design is an adaptation or extension of a style native to the region, it would appear more appropriate than would an importation completely foreign to its surroundings. To make the point to an absurd degree, no one would sanction the construction of a Swiss chalet on Miami Beach—or at least one hopes not. On the other hand, the renewed interest in Colonial and Federal heritage does not seem out of place.

In one way the resurgence of traditional home architectural forms may be charged to conservatism along with a strong assist from the cold facts of economics. Persons searching for good design in their homes may be expected to fall back on proven design—styles that have stood the test of time. They feel much more confident of the stability of a house styled in the Georgian manner than they do of a house that has a nontraditional approach. Psychologically they may feel more secure with traditional architecture; economically the values established by the market often reinforce this feeling.

Most persons feel more confident of their ability to judge traditional design. They are much less sure of themselves when it comes to evaluating contemporary architecture, and, unfortunately, it is sometimes difficult to sort out the good lasting design from the fashion of the moment.

One of the purposes of this book is to give some guidance in judgment of good design, whether traditional or nontraditional. As indicated previously, there is more to go on when we are concerned with traditional architecture. But to reiterate, *work done in the traditional manner should be done in an understanding of the traditional spirit.* Shutters do not transform an ordinary two-story house into a Colonial. To the contrary, many pre-Revolutionary houses did not have shutters, yet other characteristics define the house as Colonial. Invariably when shutters were used, they were functional; they could be used to cover the window if so desired.

224. The Garrison house of the Connecticut River Valley is distinguished by its overhanging second story in the front.

The predominant styles found in each of the five major regions have been well presented in this book. Additionally, however, I would like to discuss some variations of residential architecture which are used less frequently.

In the Northeast section of the country a number of seventeenth-century houses built in the Connecticut River Valley are distinguished by an overhanging second story in the front of the house (Fig. 224). Occasionally the second story was also extended at the gable ends, but the overhang was never used on the rear of the house. This is a variation of Colonial architecture and has been called the Garrison house, since the principle of an "overhang" was used so frequently on early fortifications in the New World. More pertinently, perhaps, it appears that this type of construction was characteristic of the part of England from which many of the Connecticut Valley artisans came.

Hand-carved drops are characteristic of the Garrison style. In modern-day examples the "drops" are sheer decoration. Originally they were the lower extensions of the four main post supports of the upper story. These houses were built around a massive central chimney, as were many other seventeenth-century houses of New England. The roof slope was somewhat steeper than that of the New England Colonial. The style is still popular in certain areas of the country.

225. A flat gambrel roof with curving eaves characterizes the Dutch Colonial house, not often seen today.

The Dutch colonists in New York and New Jersey also left their mark on the early architecture of the new country. The characteristic most closely associated with the Dutch Colonial house (Fig. 225) is its rather flat gambrel roof with the curving eaves, which often swept out over a porch along the front of the house. The attic area was sometimes lighted with small dormers.

Many homes built in this century have been called Dutch Colonial, but most examples have not truly reflected the gracious lines of their namesakes. Too often, the need for added second-floor space has caused the designer to change the conformation of the roof with the result that the house cannot be properly described as Dutch Colonial. The use of the true style is comparatively rare today.

In the chapter on the South predominant traditional styles of that region have been carefully traced and their influence on current work has been shown. On the Florida coast, though, there is a different kind of architecture. Certain forms of Mediterranean design have had some influence, but the predominant style does not seem to be clearly defined. The current architecture in this part of the country seems to have little traditional background. In the sense that contemporary architecture means the architecture of today (rather than a style with specific characteristics), most Florida architecture would probably be classified as contemporary.

In the Midwest a potpourri of styles is evident. The Colonial and the Federal or Georgian styles of the East can frequently be seen, and at one time the Greek Revival exerted a strong influence in various parts of the area.

Around the last part of the nineteenth century a particular form of design, which for lack of a generally acceptable name I call the one-and-three-quarter house or more easily the seven-quarter house, became extremely popular (Fig. 226). This name derives from the form of house that falls somewhere between the typical one-and-a-half-story and the two-story house—thus the one-and-three-quarter house.

Unlike the one-and-a-half-story house, the full second floor of the seven-quarter house is utilized, although the ceilings and roof are both sloped upward from the level of the plate of the outside wall, which is from three to five feet above the floor. Full-sized windows are used in the gable ends, and in some instances small, low windows are used along the side walls. Presumably this form evolved from the desire to make the attic area more spacious and useful.

Characteristically these houses are one room wide with a dimension of fourteen to eighteen feet, although some are two rooms wide. The smaller examples are simple rectangles; larger examples are T-shaped. The form is sometimes used as a wing on a full two-story house.

These houses can be seen everywhere in the Midwest and are particularly evident in rural areas and small towns. However, this form is seldom used in new housing, as in the Midwest today the

226. The "seven-quarter" house, common in the Midwest, utilizes the full second floor, although the ceilings are sloped.

typical small house is a one-story unit. Reduced availability of longer lumber lengths needed to balloon-frame the house may also have contributed to its decline. Recent studies of the Small Homes Council have shown, however, that the seven-quarter house can be easily constructed with a frame rigidly joined at the eaves, eliminating this consideration.

From the chapter on the Northwest it can clearly be seen that the architecture of this region probably owes less to tradition than does that of any other area of the United States. Northwest architecture is truly indigenous to the region. The style is ongoing and still developing and its characteristics have not been frozen or stereotyped. It is a style fundamentally executed in wood; the roofs are generally broad and of relatively low slope with wide overhangs; the plans are asymmetric and informal; large glass areas are evident.

There is little to add to this chapter on the Northwest, just as the chapter on the architecture of the Southwest is complete in itself. Both regions of the country have developed outstanding styles of their own. Perhaps it could be said that in the Southwest many of the styles, especially that of the desert house with its heavy massive walls, are particularly relevant to the conditions and climate of the region and the materials most readily available.

The execution of any style is as critical as its selection. The most successful styles are the simple ones. Simplicity is the key rule to good design. Good design does not require a period style; excellent housing designs are possible without reference to historical precedent. Good design grows out of the careful use of local materials with proper consideration for the climate and other conditions of the site, plus appropriate provision for the needs of the occupant of the house.

What about housing styles of the future? In my opinion, the degree to which any of the housing styles presented in this book will increase or decrease in their proportion of the total new housing mix will depend in large part on changes in our environmental living patterns, which are already predictable. These environmental changes will influence both the *type* of housing units constructed—single family or multiple family—and the *price category*, that is low- and middle-income housing, or luxury housing.

The Housing Act of 1968 provides an industry goal of twenty-six million new and rehabilitated housing units over the next ten years. During this period new household formations will rise to new highs as the World War II babies form families of their own. A majority of these young families will begin their married lives in apartment units, many of which will be of the garden-apartment variety.

Net family households throughout the 1970's will also reflect a higher proportion of the older group, sometimes referred to as the "empty nesters." With their children grown and departed, many of this group will return to apartment or other form of multifamily living because of their decreased need for living space and accommodations. Limited personal responsibility for maintenance also influences this trend toward apartment living.

Much of the same sort of reasoning, along with ever-increasing land costs, will account for the resurgence and growing importance of the town house as well. This type of housing, technically called attached housing, was at one time basic to the American scene. Today's town house, however, is anything but the attached house of yesteryear. Exciting designs and styling provide good looks in combination with all the conveniences and privacy needed. Futhermore, a more efficient, desirable utilization of land is more often found in town houses today than in most detached houses.

The shortage of relatively low-cost land suitable for urban development will, as well, force more efficient land utilization policies on the housing industry. Town houses and other forms of multiple-family housing provide answers to this problem. Perhaps I should add that because of increasing land and labor costs and other industry problems, many new industrialized construction techniques are currently being developed. Modular "stack-on" units—boxlike in configuration—sectional housing, manufactured housing, and mobile homes will eventually provide the key to mass production, and in many instances, to quality housing.

Finally, a much smaller proportion of single-family detached housing will be built. Families in the age group that creates this market will comprise a diminishing proportion of total households as compared to other age groups. The numbers of houses built to serve this group will consequently be in smaller proportion to the total.

How will architectural styles be affected by these trends? Very likely the pattern will be much the same as for today's single-family house. Those architects who tend toward eclecticism will search and find appropriate precedents in many historical styles of housing. Georgian and Colonial styles will find their way most attractively in town housing. Some architects will develop a contemporary approach to the design of these row houses with the result that the houses will be planned for today's living pattern and will also reflect the use of current materials and methods of construction.

Low-cost housing will necessarily be simpler in styling, yet this fact alone, an outgrowth of the new industrial construction system, could quickly lead to a truly indigenous new architecture of tomorrow.

GLOSSARY

ADOBE. A form of brick made from earth with firing. Common in southwestern United States.

ALCOVE. A large recess in a room (extending to the floor as distinct from a niche).

ANGLO-CLASSIC ARCHITECTURE. A term sometimes used to describe all buildings using classical or Renaissance forms or details.

APRON. A raised panel sometimes shaped and ornamented, immediately below the sill of a window or niche as if hanging therefrom. On buildings of the Renaissance and derivative styles. Also trim member immediately under projecting interior sill or stool.

ARCADE. A row of arches supported on piers or columns. A covered way, the roof of which is carried on arches similarly supported on one or both sides. A covered passage lined with shops, irrespective of its form or construction.

ASHLAR. A form of masonry.

ATRIUM. A court in the interior, open to the sky. Originally in Roman houses.

BALUSTER. One of a series of upright members which supports a handrail or capping to form a balustrade.

BALUSTRADE. The "railing" or fence protecting the edges of stairs, balconies, roofs, terraces, etc.

BAROQUE ARCHITECTURE. A late form of Renaissance architecture in which the self-imposed discipline of the earlier architects is relaxed.

BASEBOARD. See *skirting*.

BATTEN. Narrow strips of material generally used vertically to cover joints.

BAY. Space between two recurring members such as columns, roof, trusses, etc.

BAY WINDOW. A window that projects beyond the wall line, increasing the area of the apartment, the wall below it being carried down to the ground.

BEAM. A horizontal structural member generally of wood, steel, or concrete; when supporting the wall above a door or window opening, it is known as lintel.

BOND. The arrangement of blocks of building material, for example, brick or stone, in a wall making the blocks in one layer (or "course") bridge over the joints in the layer, or course, immediately below. Various bond patterns exist, such as Flemish.

BOW WINDOW. A bay or oriel window, formed in the shape of a horizontal curve, usually a segment of a circle.

BRACE. A member placed diagonally within a framework or truss to make it rigid. Braces lying in the plane of the rafters are called wind-braces, their function being to prevent wind pressure on the gables from distorting the roof.

BRIDGING. Members found between floor and ceiling joists, originally intended to stiffen and prevent twisting of structural members.

BUILDER (SPECULATIVE) HOUSING. Houses built before sale to an unknown buyer on land owned by the builder; or the builder's model home or some variation thereof, according to buyer dictates, built on land owned by the builder.

BUTTRESS. A thickening of a wall forming a vertical projection to strengthen it, for example, against the thrust of an arch, vault, or roof, or to support a heavy beam at that point.

CANOPY. A hood or rooflike structure over a niche, bed, or similar special feature, often elaborately ornamented.

CANTILEVER. A horizontal member that overhangs and carries a load a considerable distance beyond its point of support.

CAP, CAPITAL. The moldings and carved enrichment that form a finish to the top of a column, pilaster, pier, or pedestal, the term "capital" being used with reference to column and pilaster only.

CAROLEAN ARCHITECTURE. Late seventeenth-century architecture from the Restoration until the end of the century, sometimes called Late Stuart.

CASEMENT. See *window*.

CASTELLATED. Ornamented with battlements like a castle.

CAVITY WALL. See *hollow wall*.

CHAIR RAIL. A small horizontal member, generally of wood, and molded, placed so as to prevent the top of the back of a chair from damaging the wall surface.

CHAMFER. The surface obtained by cutting off a square edge at an equal angle to each face.

CHIMNEY. The channel or funnel over a fireplace or combustion chamber to carry off the products of combustion, including smoke; that part of it which projects above the roof; a "flue."

CHIMNEY BREAST. The structure, containing fireplace and flues, that is visible in the room.

CHIMNEY CAP. The molded or ornamented finish to the top of the chimney stack, but not including the chimney pot.

CHIMNEY POT. The earthenware termination of the flue, which is fixed on top of the chimney stack.

CLAPBOARD. A type of siding, usually wood, used as exterior finish in a horizontal pattern.

CLASSICAL ARCHITECTURE. The architecture of Greece and Rome of antiquity.

COLLAR BEAM. A horizontal structural member in a pitched roof connecting opposite rafters.

CONTRACT HOUSING. Housing built on land owned by the buyer, the contractural relationship being with the builder.

COPING. The protective finish to the top of a wall, for example, of parapet or gable. It is generally made with an overhanging sloping top to throw off rain, the overhang forming or being provided with a "drip."

CORNICE. The upper portion of the classical entablature; more commonly the projecting member at the top of the wall or the molding running round a room at the meeting of walls and ceiling.

COVE. A concave molding, less than a quadrant, sometimes replacing the bed molding of a cornice, joining two surfaces, for example, wall and ceiling; or, on a larger scale, disguising an overhang, as in some timber-framed houses.

CRAWL SPACE. The area below a floor between the bottom of its joists and ground. Usually about thirty inches high to permit access.

CUPOLA. A small domelike roof or lantern; a kind of turret on a roof giving light to the interior.

CURB ROOF. One in which the shape is broken on two or four sides; so called because a horizontal curb is built at the plane where the slope changes. Gambrel and mansard roofs are forms of the curb roof.

CURTAIL STEP. A step at the bottom of a flight of stairs that projects beyond the newel-post, generally finishing in a curve.

CUSTOM HOUSING. Housing built on land owned by the buyer to the buyer's specifications, often involving the services of an architect or designer.

DENTIL. One of a row of small rectangular blocks forming part of the cornice in the Ionic and Corinthian orders; also occasionally found in Doric and Composite cornices.

DOOR. A member (generally hinged) used to close an entrance to a building or room. Types: flush, paneled, batten, hollow-core, etc.

DORMER, DORMER WINDOW. A window in a sloping roof, with vertical sides and front. The front of the dormer may be a vertical continuation of the outer wall below the roof, terminating in a small gable.

DRIP. A small projection or molding beneath an overhanging member to throw rainwater clear and prevent it from creeping back and soaking into or staining the walling.

DRY WALL. A dry interior surfacing material as opposed to plaster. The most common dry wall is gypsum dry wall, which is usually ⅜″ or ½″ thick with gypsum core and heavy paper surfaces, and accepts paint or wallpaper; it is also manufactured with prefinished surfaces to simulate wood, etc.

EARLY ENGLISH ARCHITECTURE. The earliest Gothic styling in use during the thirteenth century and characterized in secular buildings by small narrow windows and steeply pointed arches.

EAVES. The overhang of a roof beyond the wall below, except at a gable. When the roof is sloping and the underside of the construction is visible from below, the eaves are said to be "open." The space between the edge of a roof and the walls is often closed in by a kind of narrow ceiling, known as the eaves "soffit."

EAVES CORNICE. A cornice formed at eaves level, extending beyond the edge of the sloping roof and often containing a rainwater gutter in its upper part.

ELEVATION. A drawing of the face or façade of a building made to scale and without perspective, showing a vertical aspect of an object or building or part of a building to indicate the exact size and relationship of its parts.

ENTABLATURE. The top member of a classic order, being a richly molded continuous lintel supported on columns. It is divided horizontally into three main parts—cornice (upper), frieze, and architrave (lower)—each with its characteristic moldings for each order, that is, Doric, Corinthian, Ionic, etc.

FACADE. A Renaissance term for the front or principal elevation of a building.

FANLIGHT. A window over a door, resembling an open fan in design; now any window in that position, irrespective of shape or pattern.

FASCIA. A vertical board fixed to the feet of rafters either for appearance or to receive a rain-water gutter.

FILLET. A narrow flat band or member separating curved moldings.

FLASHING. Usually metal (copper or aluminum), installed in sheet form to prevent water from finding a passage through construction at critical points, such as intersections between roof surfaces, at window heads, etc.

FLUSH DOOR. A modern type of door, the surfaces of which are completely flat.

FOOTINGS. Required under most foundation walls, piers, and posts to spread the load so that "house settling" is negligible.

FRENCH CASEMENT DOOR (OR WINDOW). A door or window that opens in two vertical halves without a central post or mullion and extends to floor level for use as a door.

GABLE. General reference to the pedimentry (triangular shape) end of a roof, as distinguished from a hip-gabled roof.

GABLET. A little gable.

GAMBREL ROOF. A "curb" or mansard roof with only two of the four opposite sides in a broken slope. It is therefore a gabled curb roof.

GEORGIAN ARCHITECTURE. Generally the period from George I to the Regency. See *Regency architecture.*

GIRDER. A strong beam supporting other beams or joists and binding them together.

GLAZING. The fitting of glass in windows, doors, skylights, screens, etc. Double glazing: several panes of glass with air space between, that is, (1) storm sash, (2) hermetically sealed at edges with air space between, called insulating glass.

GOTHIC ARCHITECTURE. The architecture of the Middle Ages, the most familiar characteristic of which is the pointed arch.

GREEK REVIVAL ARCHITECTURE. A style influenced by renewed interest in Greek classical architecture. The Greek Revival did not make rapid progress until after 1790; Greek detail was shortly after to be found on many new town houses. Ionic as well as Doric columns were used, especially in porches, which were the main embellishment on the rather plain houses. Other characteristics were a general "squat" appearance, low attic stories, low-pitched pediments, windows set in plain shallow recesses, sometimes with low segmental heads, fillets and moldings with very slight projection.

GUTTER. A channel for collecting rainwater, especially from a roof, and conveying it to pipes through which it flows to a drain or the ground.

HALF-TIMBER CONSTRUCTION. A system of timber framing utilizing widely spaced irregular timbers enclosing vaguely rectangular panels of masonry (often covered with stucco). The lower stories are usually of masonry such as stonework, and the upper stories or perhaps only the walls of the gables are usually framed in timber.

HEAD. Upper part of a door, window, etc., of an opening in a wall. The top member of a frame.

HIP. The meeting line of adjoining slopes of a pitched roof, at an external angle of a building, dormer, etc.

HIPPED ROOF. A pitched roof, the end of which is also sloped back, meeting the side slopes in a pair of hips.

HOLLOW WALL, CAVITY WALL. The modern ten-inch wall formed of two "withes," "leaves," or "skins" of four-inch masonry with a two-inch air space between. To obtain stability, the two thin walls are linked at regular intervals by metal wall ties. Hollow walls are also built of any suitable material in the thicknesses needed.

INSULATION. A material, usually mineral wool, fiber glass, or foamed plastic, placed between warm and cold areas to reduce heat transfer.

JACK RAFTER. A short rafter, used especially in hip roofs.

JACOBEAN ARCHITECTURE. The architecture of the reign of James I, the last phase of Gothic building in England in which the Tudor style expanded, coarsened, and died.

JALOUSIE. A blind or shutter; in particular, a hinged or sliding shutter having sloping slats arranged to exclude rain while admitting air. Often made of glass slats in metal frame.

JAMB. The side of an opening in a wall, for example, for a door or window; that part of the post, frame, or lining secured or attached to it; the side (or "cheek") of a fireplace opening.

LANDING. A level space between two flights of stairs or steps; also that part of the floor at the top of the stair.

LANTERN. A kind of turret on a roof, with windows in the sides to light the interior below, or with louvers to provide ventilation; a similar structure on the top of a dome.

LEADED GLAZING. The filling-in of openings for windows in a wall, partition, screen, etc., with small pieces of glass joined by narrow strips of lead to form a large sheet.

LIGHT. A window. Now understood to refer to one of the main subdivisions of a window.

LINTEL. The horizontal structural member that supports the walling over an opening, or spans between two adjacent piers or columns.

LOGGIA. A covered outdoor space for sitting or walking, open on one or more sides; generally attached to or forming part of the structure of the house. A covered arcade or colonnade similarly placed.

MANSARD ROOF. A roof form that runs up from all four plates, instead of two as in the gambrel. A pitched roof with two slopes each of four sides, the lower being steeper than the upper.

MANTEL. The beam or lintel supporting the chimney breast over a fireplace.

MASONRY. The craft of working or building with stone, brick, precast concrete, and artificial stone.

MEDIEVAL ARCHITECTURE. The architecture of the period between the Norman conquest and the Reformation. The architecture of the Middle Ages. (See *Gothic architecture*).

MITRE. The joint made between two long narrow pieces of material of similar profile when brought together at an angle as at the corner of a picture frame.

MODERN ARCHITECTURE. In a strict sense, architecture in which all historical styles of building and ornamentation are discarded. Le Corbusier, Gropius, and Frank Lloyd Wright were among the early proponents. Easily recognized: flat or low-sloped roofs, severity of treatment, and large window spaces. More broadly, contemporary, not based on the traditional.

MODULE. A unit dimension. Modular systems are being tried in modern housing in the hope of achieving economies through the resulting rationalization and standardization of building components and the elimination of waste.

MOLDING. The manipulation or working of a plane surface to produce parallel stripes of light and shade, sharply differentiated or graded as required. They may be formed on the edge or face of a member (on the solid) or as separate strips which are fixed (applied or planted) to produce a similar effect.

MOSAIC. A form of decoration in which a picture or design is made by cementing together very small pieces of different-colored stone, marble, glass, etc., on the surface of a floor, wall, vault, or ceiling.

MULLION. An upright post or similar member dividing a window into two or more units or "lights," each of which may be divided into panes.

MUNTIN. A member separating panes of glass in a window or door.

NEWEL. An upright structural member in a wooden staircase into which the handrails and strings (see *staircase*) are framed.

NICHE. A shallow recess in a wall, pier, buttress, etc., shaped and ornamented in the architectural manner of the time for the placement of a statue, vase, or urn.

NOSING. The rounded edge of the tread of a step which projects beyond the riser.

OWNER-BUILT HOUSING. Usually where the owner acts as his own "general contractor" and subcontracts the work to be done, for example, carpentry, electricity, plumbing, etc.

PALLADIAN ARCHITECTURE. The basic English interpretation of Italian Renaissance architecture, based on the works and books of the Italian architect Andrea Palladio (1518–1580), first introduced by Inigo Jones in the early seventeenth century in England. Characteristic Palladian features are strictly formal three-part grouping of the house comprising the main central block with portico and two often widely spaced wings connected to it by single-story passages, screens, or colonnades; the use of a large order (usually that of the portico) extending through the two principal stories of the façade of the central block, using the ground-floor wall as a pedestal; small orders supporting arches in the spaces between larger columns carrying an entablature, used as a decoration around a door or window.

PARAPET. A low wall at the edge of a roof, generally formed by an upward extension of the wall below; a similar erection on a bridge, gallery, balcony, etc.

PARGING. Thin coat of plastering to smooth off rough brick or stone walls.

PARQUETRY. Geometrical pattern of thin pieces of hardwood to form a floor.

PAVILION. A decorative garden house.

PEDESTAL. The base upon which a statue, vase, etc., is placed. The support upon which a column stands. It consists of cap, die, and plinth, its dimensions and proportions being related to those of the column that stands upon it, that is, one fourth of the combined height of column and entablature.

PEDIMENT.   The triangular low-pitched gable end of a Greek or Roman temple with characteristic cornice moldings and ornament, which was supported by a row of columns.

PIER.   A solid vertical mass of walling between two openings. A similar free-standing mass supporting one side of an arch or one end of a beam, lintel, or girder.

PILASTER.   The projecting part of a square column that is attached to a wall and finished with the same cap and base as a free-standing column, adjusted to suit the rectangular shape.

PITCH.   The steepness of a sloping roof, generally expressed as an angle or as a ratio between height and span.

PLAN.   Drawing or diagram, to scale, of interior arrangement of a house or building showing the signs and disposition of its parts.

PLATE.   A horizontal member at the top of the wall frame, generally supporting the roof rafters and the second-floor joints.

PORTE COCHERE.   A projecting porch over an entranceway large enough for people to alight from a vehicle and enter the building under cover.

PUGGING.   Material laid between the beams or joists supporting a floor above and a ceiling below to reduce the passage of sound.

PURLIN.   A horizontal beam in a roof which supports the rafters.

QUARREL.   One of the small diamond-shaped panes of glass in a leaded light window.

QUARRY TILE.   A small square clay tile used for flooring or paving.

QUEEN ANNE STYLE.   Time and period of house intermediate between Carolean and Georgian.

QUOIN.   Bricks or stones forming exterior corners, brought forward or otherwise emphasized.

RAFTER.   One of a series of structural timbers rising from eaves to ridge which support the covering of a pitched roof.

REGENCY ARCHITECTURE.   Two kinds: (1) Greek Revival of the late eighteenth century and (2) Romantic movement with Gothic overtones, usually in small semidetached villa form.

RENAISSANCE ARCHITECTURE.   Derived from the architecture of the Renaissance in Italy. Still a persuasive influence on some designers today.

RIDGE.   The top of a roof that rises to an acute angle.

RISER.   The vertical surface, or the piece of material forming it, between one tread and the next in a stair.

ROCOCO.   A form of decoration, somewhat French in feeling; a merging of Chinese and Gothic motifs in interior decoration.

ROOF.   Structure covering space between top of the walls, providing shelter. Various roof forms in existence, such as shed or lean-to, gable, hip, gambrel, mansard, deck, curb.

ROOF TRUSS.   A framework of structural members arranged and jointed in such a way as to support the weight of a roof covering and resist the pressure of wind and weight of snow upon it. Roof trusses carry horizontal members (purlins) spanning between them, which in turn support the actual roof, and may be supported on walls, piers, or individual stanchions.

RUBBLE.   Uncut stone or roughly shaped stone used in walls, foundations, or older houses.

SASH.   A framework containing a sheet or sheets of glass, as in a door, window, skylight, etc. In particular, that in a double-hung sliding sash window.

SHINGLE.   Many varieties for roof and sidewall finish. Sawn-wood shingles are cut to regular square-cut shape. Hand-split are more irregular with greater surface texture. Numerous other types made of asbestos, asphalt, cement, fiber glass, clay tile, etc.

SILL. The horizontal member immediately above and supported by the foundation wall or piers; also, the lower member of exterior door frames and window frames.

SKIRTING. A horizontal member, generally a thin wooden board, fixed to the bottom of a wall or partition where it meets the floor as a protective finish.

SOFFIT. Covering over space between edge of overhanging roof and the vertical wall surface.

SPAN. The distance between the supports of a beam, girder, arch, truss, etc.

STAIRCASE. The framed-up structure of a wooden stair comprising treads and risers let in to the upstanding bearers known as strings, and supported by vertical posts, or newels, as desired. Many varieties with or without balustrades.

STUD. One of the vertical wooden posts that stand on the sill or sole plate and support the head of a timber-framed partition. Also used to describe posts of other materials, such as steel or aluminum.

TERRAZZO. A concrete pavement used for floors in which cement mortar and small pieces of colored marble are combined, cast, and then ground to produce a smooth, polished surface.

THATCH. A covering for pitched roofs in use from very early times, consisting of a thick layer of reeds, straw, or heather.

TUDOR ARCHITECTURE. Architecture of the time of Tudor monarchs, 1485–1603, in which English house building reached its peak of magnificence. Grouped windows, many chimneys, large fireplaces, flexible plan, interior and exterior flat arches, lead-glazed windows, and oak paneling are among its characteristics.

TURRET. A small towerlike structure built against the side of a building or into an angle in castles and Tudor houses.

VALLEY. The internal angle formed at the meeting of two sloping sections of roof.

VAPOR BARRIER. A material usually in sheet form (often as part of an insulation device) designed to prevent water vapor from infiltrating one side of a wall, floor, or ceiling due to temperature differences on the opposing side.

VAULT. An arched roof or ceiling constructed of brick or stone; an underground storeroom; a cellar; an undercroft.

VERTICAL BOARD. A term usually applied to wood members applied vertically. When individual boards, they are usually of redwood or cedar. Joints are often matched (tongue and grooved) or covered with battens. Also simulated by using patterned sheets four feet wide of plywood, hardboard, or metal (board and batten siding).

VICTORIAN ARCHITECTURE. A conglomeration of past styles and their embellishments selected for the feelings they aroused, an outgrowth of the essentially romantic Victorian age.

WAINSCOT. An early name for the wooden lining of the walls of a room, before true paneling was introduced. The term was also used for wall paneling generally, the oak used for paneling, and paneling up to dado height.

WINDOW. An opening in an outside wall to admit light and air; a frame of wood or metal filled with glass, either fixed shut or made to open. There are two types of opening window in common use: the casement, in which the glazed frame is hinged, generally on one side to open outward, and the double-hung vertical sliding window. In the latter, a pair of glazed sashes slide up and down in front of each other. Other forms of windows: picture windows, jalousie windows, sliding windows, projected windows, and awning windows.

ILLUSTRATION CREDITS

HOUSES OF THE SOUTH

Preface
photo.   Courtesy, Library of Congress
1. Home of Mr. and Mrs. Fred Scheer, Atlanta
2. Home of Mr. and Mrs. I. Wilen, Atlanta
3. Upson House, Athens, Ga. Courtesy, Library of Congress
4. Courtesy, Library of Congress
5. A Colonial Williamsburg Photograph
6. The Dodd House, La Grange, Ga. Courtesy, Library of Congress
7. Courtesy, Library of Congress
9. Home of Dr. John Bottomy, Atlanta
10. Home of Mr. and Mrs. Jones Beene, Athens, Tenn.
14–23. Courtesy, Library of Congress
25–26, 30–39. Colonial Williamsburg Photographs
40. Home of Mr. and Mrs. Julian LeCraw, Atlanta
42. Home of Mr. and Mrs. Henry D. Norris, Atlanta. Clyde May, photographer, Atlanta
43–44. Hedrich-Blessing, photographer, Chicago
45. Name of owner withheld
46. Home of Mrs. John O. Chiles, Atlanta
47. Home of Mr. and Mrs. Henry D. Norris, architect, Atlanta. A Clyde May Photograph
48. Home of Mr. and Mrs. Henry D. Norris, architect, Atlanta. A Clyde May Photograph
49. A modern house designed by the author, Henry D. Norris. Courtesy, *Better Homes & Gardens*
50. A modern house designed by the author, Henry D. Norris. Courtesy, *Better Homes & Gardens*
51. Home of R. A. Siegel
52. Home of General William R. Woodward
53. Home of Dr. George Holloway
54. Home of Richard L. Hull

55. Home of J. A. Black
56. Home of Guy H. Schull
57. Home of Alvin B. Cates, Jr.
58. Home of Paul A. Duke
59. Home of Neal C. Peavy
60. Home of Ben P. Jones
61. Home of Dr. Thomas Dillon

HOUSES OF THE NORTHWEST

Preface
photo.   Wm. Shadel House, Medina, Wash., John Anderson & Assoc., architects
62. Hugh Stratford, photographer, Mountlake Terrace, Wash.
63. Storey Cottages, Ellsworth Storey, architect
64. Hedrich-Blessing, photographer, Chicago
65. John Anderson, photographer, Bellevue, Wash.
66. Chas. R. Pearson, photographer, Edmonds, Wash.
67. Hugh Stratford, photographer, Mountlake Terrace, Wash.
68. John Anderson & Assoc., architects
69. John Anderson, photographer, Bellevue, Wash.
70. Chas. R. Pearson, photographer, Edmonds, Wash.
71. John Anderson, photographer, Bellevue, Wash.
72. R. Komen House, Juanta, Wash., John Anderson & Assoc., architects
73. Dudley, Hardin & Yang, photographers, John Anderson & Assoc., architects
74. G. Shupe House, Bellevue, Wash.
75–76. Ernest Fortescue, photographer, Kirkland, Wash.
77–78. Courtesy, *Better Homes & Gardens*
79–80. John Anderson, photographer, Bellevue, Wash.
81. Ernest Fortesque, photographer, Kirkland, Wash.
82–85. Wm. Shadel House, John Anderson & Assoc., architects

INDEX

RICHARD M. BALLINGER has long been a student of the housing industry. With a background in mechanical engineering and architecture, he has for the past seventeen years been in the publishing field, where his work has been closely related to housing. First with *House and Home,* then Time, Inc., publications, he has been a marketing manager for *Better Homes & Gardens* for the last nine years. His activities have given him an intimate knowledge of the fields of housing, architecture, construction, and building products. He is a member of the National Housing Council, the marketing committee of the National Association of Home Builders, and the board of directors of the National Home Improvement Council, and he has recently been engaged as a consultant in low- and middle-income housing by conventional builders and home manufacturers. He and his wife, Nancy, live in Wilton, Connecticut, and his two children, June and Chuck, are away at college.